A Sociological Study of Street Children in Ghana

Victims of Kinship Breakdown and Rural-Urban Migration

A Sociological Study of Street Children in Ghana

Victims of Kinship Breakdown and Rural-Urban Migration

Vivian Amantana

With a Foreword by

Stephen G. Gibbons

The Edwin Mellen Press
Lewiston•Queenston•Lampeter

Library of Congress Cataloging-in-Publication Data

Amantana, Vivian.
A sociological study of street children in Ghana : victims of kinship breakdown and rural-urban migration / Vivian Amantana ; with a foreword by Stephen G. Gibbons.
p. cm.
Includes bibliographical references and index.
ISBN-13: 978-0-7734-1606-2 (hardcover)
ISBN-10: 0-7734-1606-4 (hardcover)
1. Street children--Ghana--Social conditions. 2. Child welfare--Ghana. 3. Rural-urban migration--Ghana. 4. Ghana--Social conditions. 5. Ghana--Economic conditions. I. Title.
HV887.G4A43 2011
362.77'569209667--dc23
2011020165

hors série.

A CIP catalog record for this book is available from the British Library.

Front cover photo: A Ghanaian family returning home after an afternoon of work in the fields.
Credit: © Victor Englebert

The Edwin Mellen Press
Box 450
Lewiston, New York
USA 14092-0450

The Edwin Mellen Press
Box 67
Queenston, Ontario
CANADA L0S 1L0

The Edwin Mellen Press, Ltd.
Lampeter, Ceredigion, Wales
UNITED KINGDOM SA48 8LT

Printed in the United States of America

"My mother was the most beautiful woman I ever saw. All I am, I owe to my Mother. I attribute all my success in life to the moral, intellectual and physical education I received from her."

—George Washington, the first president of the United States of America

To my mother, Mrs. Ernestina Bimunka Djokotoe, and street children across the world

Contents

Figures

1. One of the open markets in central Accra. These urban market places often double as shopping precincts and bus terminals.
2. A rural household consisting of a number of units that house the members of the family. In the foreground is a collection of firewood used as the main source of energy for cooking.
3. Southern rural folks at the village borehole, which serves as their source of water for domestic use.
4. A northern Ghana community. Homes built from mud with thatched roofs are typical of this region.
5. A young man in a neighborhood of Accra is seen here transporting a load of farm produce by means of a two-wheeled cart. Most of the male migrants on the streets in Accra offer services this kind of to the vendors.
6. The Buipe field research liaison flanked by two northern women who are mothers of some members of the participants.
7. A closer look at the open market in Accra. The structures in the background are stalls that house the vendors, most of whom sell farm produce and fish.
8. Drawing of a grave by a South African street child.
   Courtesy: Jill Swart, 1990.

Tables

Foreword

As long as there have been cities, street children have probably also existed: runaways, throwaways, and homeless youth populating urban areas. However, studies of these children, and explanations for why they end up on the streets, come largely from the developed world. Dr. Vivian Amantana's study of Ghanaian street children obviously departs from this mode of inquiry. Moreover, her work is conducted from an insider's perspective and utilizes the words of the children themselves as the source of her very rich data.

The serious socioeconomic implications of the street children phenomenon are inescapable and transcend geographical and cultural boundaries. This is a social "pandemic," as well as an equal-opportunity danger for children around the world. As such, a wide variety of prevention and/or intervention programs have sprung up worldwide, which, depending on the country, work at the local, national, or international level. Some of these programs are conventional social services reacting to the problem, others are proactive and innovative, and many are purely law enforcement oriented. Regardless of the approach, the intention of each of these programs or measures is to eventually mitigate or ameliorate the occurrence of street children in the targeted area. Although such programs are aggressively pursuing this objective, it is apparent that the phenomenon of street children remains intractable as is evidenced by the fact that worldwide, the number of street children continues to grow.

So why is it that these programs seem to have relatively negligible results? How is it that the problem seems to intensify with no respite in sight? Does this undesired result suggest these programs may have only a nominal effect or perhaps none at all? Could it be that these programs fail to identify the actual causes of this problem or are not funded at the level necessary for success? Is it possible that these programs may even have the unintended consequence of aggravating this phenomenon? There is also the problem where, in many instances, prevention or intervention programs have relied on data gathered in the Western world to develop and structure programs in developing countries. Although such efforts may have good intentions and are due in large part to the lack of research and data in developing countries, it is not surprising that such efforts often meet with limited success. Perhaps an even greater concern is the application of a law enforcement approach in some developing countries. These approaches are usually not based on research at all and usually culminate in the criminalization of these children, who then sometimes pay the ultimate price for their "criminality"—summary executions.

Dr. Amantana's work, based on an emic, or insider's, perspective within the social, cultural, and economic framework of the Ghanaian community, seeks to avoid these problems and issues. Her work synthesizes some answers to the nagging questions posed above and ultimately provides some guidance to the international effort of slowing down and eventually eliminating this social hemorrhage, at least within the African subregion south of the Sahara. This book unravels some of the reasons children migrate to urban streets rather than staying "home," and is based on the experience of the Ghanaian street children, told in their own words. As Dr. Amantana's work reveals some of the causes underlying this phenomenon in Ghana, the reader will realize that there are factors, both obvious and obscure, that are genuine and pivotal and that contribute to the understanding of the migration of children from rural to urban areas. Furthermore, although this research is based in Ghana, the contribution it makes to our understanding of this international issue, particularly as it applies to the developing world, cannot be overstated. By allowing the children to explain, in their own words, the reasons for their migration, Dr. Amantana allows the reader to see into the world of these children, while at the same time her explanations for why they migrate suggest programmatic and policy changes that could easily contribute to the mitigation of a phenomenon that is harmful to individuals, families, communities, and the society at large.

Stephen G. Gibbons, PhD
Professor and Chair of the Criminal Justice Department
Western Oregon University

Preface

She listened in astonishment, then asked, "But where are the street children?" then added, "There are no street children in this youth day shelter." This was Adjoa's response when, in 1996, I met and interacted with her during my visit to the Catholic Action for Street Children facility located in the James Town suburb of Accra, Ghana's administrative capital. Adjoa's response was nothing more than routine, coming from a youngster who obviously appeared oblivious to reality and was probably representative of the false impression within this cohort. Prior to this visit, I had spent a few months at this facility as part of my effort to earn a bachelor's degree in social work from the University of Ghana, West Africa, and also as a staging ground to launch my career. The program was to ultimately provide me with a real-world scenario, far remote from what I envisioned prior to assuming this placement. I was of the impression that the program would take the form of an office setting, where I would sit behind a desk, meet with clients, and counsel and help rehabilitate them based on my skills and in accordance with the professional code of ethics. I felt very confident about this placement and looked forward to the program knowing that this was an opportunity to put into practice the course work (such as the theories of delinquency, causes of youth homelessness, and approach to handling troubled youth from a professional standpoint) I offered at the university's top-notch social work program. It became abundantly clear from the very beginning, as I made my way into the facility, that the road was going to be intense and treacherous. Only at that moment did I realize I had ventured into the belly of the beast via a one-way street.

What appeared to be a dream soon fizzled, and I was now in touch with reality as I made my way through the compound on my first day at the facility. As I was led across the compound, I constantly reached for the address in my purse to ensure I had not strayed elsewhere. The tour of the facility left me motionless, and I began to wonder where the counseling and medication units were located. The situation soon took an even more disturbing turn when I became embedded with the fieldworkers for the very first time, to track these children as they wandered the streets of Accra in search of jobs. This stunning and chilling revelation was to become one that would constantly dazzle my imagination and provide me with such vital and real understanding of the world of the "street." The shelter was casual and appeared to be a place where these street children would retreat during the day for food and a place of convenience. While these children interacted freely, played games, and sometimes became strident in the process, the shelter also offered opportunities to help develop various vocational skills. I would later get the opportunity to directly interact with these youngsters, and soon learned that aside from the basic training given at the shelter, limited formal education was offered on occasion.

As the story unfolded and the picture of the world in which these kids treaded wearily became more and more vivid, I began to understand the uniqueness of Ghanaian street children, the driving force behind their plight, and the streets they roamed. This program provided the inescapable evidence that the Western world's definition of a street child could not be directly applied to the Ghanaian situation. My visit to the youth shelter, which obviously was crafted as a purely academic exercise, soon became the reset button for me personally and professionally with special reference to the factors that spawned homeless youth and the need for intervention.

I had settled for daily interactions with these kids in a less-than-professional fashion and was getting to understand them and their stories in greater detail as I spent part of the time engaging these kids in conversations that were mutual and candid. One of the youngsters, Adjoa, a very confident, dark-skinned young lady with beautiful bright eyes, was drawn to me when I arrived at the shelter. Adjoa was very voluble and outgoing, and her presence was routinely felt in the shelter. My interactions with Adjoa grew with time, and it became evident she was a pretty, smart, and curious girl who posed intelligent questions. My interaction with Adjoa was one of many that I frequently had with the youngsters who came to the shelter during working hours of the day.

A follow-up trip to a few of the villages in Northern Ghana after the completion of the program was aimed at meeting with parents of some of these street children and listening first hand to their stories. This interaction provided the other dimension of the phenomenon of rural–urban migration. My conversations with these families demonstrated that the term "street kids" was a misnomer and failed to provide a fair, specific, and direct definition of this phenomenon. In my quest to get a more detailed understanding of this phenomenon, which is simply labeled "streetism," I proceeded to mine information by engaging in a second round of interactions with street children in the northern and southern belts of the country. The information gathered from the perspectives of these children was very illuminating and revealed to me the inadequacies in the level of understanding of this phenomenon from the academic standpoint. On the basis of this, I began to develop a strong sense of duty to individuals like Adjoa and to narrate their story in their own words to the outside world as we dialogue the Ghanaian phenomenon. This book is expected to serve as a rare window of opportunity for the reader by providing a better understanding of this phenomenon in Ghana.

Vivian Amantana

Acknowledgments

Academics make their careers out of the never-ending process of learning and teaching, which means my career was created and is sustained by the help of many teachers at every turn. I acknowledge the crucial roles played by all of these people mentioned here in educating me in various ways that got me here and constantly reminding me how much I have been given in my life.

My special thanks go to my husband, Dr. Adams Amantana, who was unrelenting at every step of the way as I pursued this goal. You are not only a loving husband, but one of my greatest teachers and mentors. You had faith in my ability to complete this undertaking when I had difficulty seeing it. I can truly say that this book would not exist without your efforts. Thanks for the sleepless nights you spent proofreading and editing every bit of this book. This work is yours just as much as mine. You remain a faithful friend, a wonderful loving partner, and obviously an important part of my life. Adams, I appreciate you so much, and my gratitude to you is endless. To my daughter Elita, thanks so much for filling my life with so much joy and reminding me why I do all of this.

From the beginning of my academic journey, I had the best of my lessons from my parents, Mr. Cephas Kwaku Ashiaby Djokotoe and Ernestina Bimunka Djokotoe, who were my earliest cheerleaders. They presented me with a big, wide world of opportunities and enabled me to be my authentic self by allowing me to navigate it myself, with their unconditional support at every step. My mother blazed this trail as the first woman from Northern Ghana to make it to the university level in Ghana against all odds; she showed me I can achieve anything I set my mind on. My mom also did most of the preparatory work for my fieldwork and served as a liaison between me and the families during data collection. Mom, you are my biggest role model, and your impact on my life is immeasurable. I will continue to cherish your love, guidance, and dedication to my education. My deep appreciation goes to my parents-in-law; my sisters Edna, Diana, Hilda, and Sylvia; and to all my friends for their love and support, especially Mercy Luguterah, who ventured with me into this area of research; Wilma Hull, who continues to remind me of the importance of service to the underprivileged; and Patty Parnell, who has been a great cheerleader.

My academic introduction into this area was prompted by Dr. Nana Araba Apt Van Ham, the then chair of the Social Work Program at the University of Ghana, Legon. You instilled in me the importance of applying the knowledge gained in class to the field, which resulted in the conception of this study. Your trailblazing work in bringing the plight of street children in Ghana to the fore made it possible for this study to be completed. A significant part of this work was accomplished during my graduate studies at Oregon State University, where I benefited from the excellent guidance of my professors. I express sincere gratitude to Dr. Samuel Vuchinich, my major professor and mentor. I appreciate his tremendous support and guidance for me every step of the way. I am also grateful to Dr. Richard Mitchel, Dr. Patricia Moran, Dr. Leslie Richards, and Dr. Larry Roper, who offered vital support and feedback. To my colleagues at Western Oregon University, especially Dr. Stephen Scheck, Dr. Stephen Gibbons, and Dr. Peter Callero, and to Dr. Charles Quist-Adade of Kwantlen Polytechnic University in Canada, thanks so much for your tremendous contributions to this process.

This work would not have been born if not for the cooperation of the Catholic Action for Street Children and Tizaa Action Aid, the nongovernmental organizations (NGOs) that served as a link between me and the participants. Treading into this territory was scary for me, but, thanks to Brother Jos Van Dinther at Catholic Action for Street Children, I am at this stage today. I consider you my first teacher in this research area because you accepted me, gave me my first steps into this area of study in a safe way, and gave me the opportunity to work with your knowledgeable staff during my initial fieldwork. Agnes Chiravira at Tizaa was instrumental in making my fieldwork in Tamale possible. Thanks for being a true champion in the fight to help these brave children on the street. Finally, to the brave street children and the families who shared their stories, thank you for providing a voice to all street children in Ghana.

Chapter One
Introduction

The phenomenon of children on urban streets in the Western world has been well studied, and there is consensus among numerous researchers that the presence of youths on urban streets constitutes a global problem with serious social and economic implications (Epstein, 1996; Mufume, 2000; Raffaelli et al., 2001; Symons & Smith, 1995). In fact, the United Nations Children's Fund estimates that over three hundred million children live on urban streets worldwide, most of them in the developing world (Beauchemin, 1999). Available statistics now place the number of street children in Accra (Ghana's administrative capital) alone at approximately twenty thousand (Shanahan, 2002), constituting a little less than half of the country's total street children (World Health Organization, 2000).

Unlike the Western world where this phenomenon has been widely studied, it was not until the 1990s when preliminary studies on the Ghanaian situation begun to emerge (Van Dinther, 2000). In addition, the fact that academics are quick to extrapolate data from the Western world to the Ghanaian situation has further contributed to the lack of studies in the Ghanaian context, further placing a limitation on the generation of data. It is against this background that there is an apparent lack of adequate and aggressive government-run social programs to address this problem (Beauchemin, 1999), as is also the case in most African countries (Mufume, 2000). A study by Beauchemin (1999) has shown that existing correction programs under the auspices of the Ghanaian government to a large extent align with the unfavorable public perceptions and misconceptions that usually culminate in criminalization, summary convictions, and possible incarceration or even executions (McCreery, 2001; Jahangir, 2002). From these studies, it is apparent that the government of Ghana gives recognition to street children as a concern but lacks a real understanding of the causes of this phenomenon and, therefore, takes the position that it is based on choice rather than necessity that these children leave home for urban streets (Beauchemin, 1999).

Existing data show that rural–urban migration plays a major role in the presence of children on urban streets in Ghana, and factors such as rural underdevelopment, the lure of urbanization, adventure seeking, peer pressure, parental abuse and neglect, and unfavorable traditional practices in rural communities have contributed to this migration (Beauchemin, 1999). However, these studies are based on an etic or outsider's perspective, and therefore these findings may fall short of revealing the remaining strata underlying this phenomenon. This etic standpoint can also be found within the Ghanaian public that has wrongly embraced the misnomer "streetism," which tends to reinforce the misconceptions of the Ghanaian society.

On the basis of this, it is imperative to conduct research from an emic, or insider's, perspective to provide a better understanding of the complexities involved in these social phenomena (Glesne & Peshkin, 1992). Hence, it is extremely important to conduct studies that explore this phenomenon in a similar fashion in order to determine the remote or fundamental factors that tend to drive these children onto urban streets. Diversi (1998) and Finley (1999) have demonstrated that there is the need to incorporate the voices of street children into the discourse centered on their lives on urban streets by evaluating the rationale for their decisions, based on their own perspectives. Consequently, this study was designed to utilize data generated from the perspective of these street children that is considered adequate enough to determine the remote causes of rural–urban migration within this cohort and the urban street experience in their own words. This book is designed to put forward in-depth findings from an insider's perspective, based on the thoughts of the Ghanaian street child beyond what is readily recognizable. The application of academic interpretations that are theory driven in this edition will ultimately provide a thorough evaluation of this phenomenon and is expected to offer adequate pathways toward a fairly comprehensive, attainable, effective, and sustainable intervention program(s).

It must also be emphasized that as NGOs continue to reach out to street children in an effort to build both public and stakeholders' support, there is the urgent need to clearly identify and understand the specific factors that engender the presence of children on urban streets in Ghana. It is expected that this effort will provide a viable formula needed to confront this growing phenomenon.

This text focuses on youth who live on urban streets in Ghana, describing in their own words their reasons for making a home on urban streets, however temporarily, and seeking to provide detail from an insider's perspective the individual's own account describing the significance they attach to their decision to migrate.

Ekua is a seventeen-year-old girl who migrated from her rural hometown of Suhum to Accra and has been on the street for one and a half years as of the time of the interview. Ekua arrived in Accra at the encouragement of a friend who is affiliated with a food vendor resident in Accra, with the goal of securing a job with this entrepreneur. Upon arrival, Ekua was offered a job, raising her hopes of a brighter future and pushing her a step closer to her dream of becoming a hair stylist. This dream soon turned into a nightmare as seven months passed without any remuneration, in sharp contrast to the terms of the contract. Frustration began to grow, and Ekua had no option but to resume the treacherous journey toward achieving a better life. Ekua finally parted ways with her employer with absolutely nothing to show for good work done, and except for what appeared to be her enduring spirit, perseverance, and courage, she walked an intense trail in anticipation of a better opportunity. Ekua tells her story in her own words:

> I arrived here in Accra in the company of my friend in search of job opportunities. My friend indicated he knew someone here in Accra who is a vendor at the market and suggested we go and work for the vendor. Fortunately, I secured a job with this vendor for about seven months. The contract was that, I will be paid seven thousand cedis for a day's work. My employer came to me weeks later and indicated the terms of the contract needed to be modified and that she will offer four thousand cedis per day by virtue of the fact that she provided me with shelter and food. Seven months passed without one cedi. Clearly, someone was shifting the goal post here. So I decided to abdicate and find another opportunity elsewhere.
>
> I anticipated that I could work there for a while, and earn and save up enough money to train as hair stylist within the city. My plan was to own a salon after acquiring the skills. Earlier in the process, I remember my friend indicating to me about how much I could earn working here, so I thought there was an incentive in migrating. My friend worked for a woman who ran an eatery, and I am witness to how well she did. Unfortunately I was sent to work for a different woman who simply exploited me. A lot of girls come from rural communities to work for her. She offered every one of them what was due them except me, and I attribute this to nepotism because all the other girls migrated from the same rural location of which the vendor is a native.

Ekua is one of two children in her family. She reports that her father left for a neighboring French-speaking country and has since failed to contact the rest of the family, the beginning of what will eventually become nothing but a fractured home. Ekua's mother still lives in Suhum, but their inability to communicate further complicates her situation. In the midst of her grim challenge, Ekua receives information indicating her brother, just like her, roams the streets of Accra, and she looks forward to meeting him for the first time after such a long time. Ekua's mother is very much aware Ekua lives in Accra but is completely oblivious to the kind of job Ekua may have secured. Ekua has decided to keep it that way and not make any disclosure. Prior to her departure, Ekua enrolled in a village elementary school and all those years knew very well how little the rural environment could offer to the younger generation, and consequently was of the impression that formal education could not provide any way forward. Ekua was at a crossroad and had to make a quick decision, and when the opportunity showed up at the doorstep, the response was a spontaneous yes.

Ekua disclosed that she left home against her mother's wishes, as the allure of the city was so overwhelming that no amount of persuasion could sway her. Ekua indicated she would not have gone this direction if some form of support had been available back home to provide her with the much-needed momentum in the right direction. Seven months of toil had gone down the drain, and now Ekua finds herself on the streets of Accra anxiously looking forward to a bright moment at every sunrise. Ekua has stated that life on the streets is testing beyond imagination, and every day brings new challenges as the ascent gets even more intense and hope diminishes at an even greater pace.

Ekua indicated that going into the night on a virtually empty stomach was becoming a predictable occurrence as one knew that there was one way to dinner, and that was in finding some menial work before the close of the day. For Ekua, the days appeared short and the nights very long, and anxiety mounted with time. Asked how she is able to sustain herself, Ekua paused and responded "Hmm . . . as for food, I eat when I am lucky to find some money, otherwise I go to sleep hungry." Ekua indicated she goes to a youth shelter where first aid or basic medical care is provided in the event of an injury and/or malaria infection. Here is how Ekua put it in her own words: "When I am ill, I come here to the shelter. There is a nurse here who gives us first aid. It is a free service."

According to Ekua, the children will huddle at night and during the day; they roam the streets of Accra in desperate search of ever-receding job opportunities. Ekua talks about the system on the streets, where the older and athletic street boys secure spots in the market stalls, which appear safe, and rent them out to other street children every night, a clear case of survival of the fittest. As incentive, these older boys become sentinels against other street youth who may have the tendency to steal and harass their group. Ekua expressed profound concern about the level of public misconception and wished the public would appreciate that they are human and are on the streets of Accra to earn a livelihood. Here is Ekua's response when asked how the public perceives of their presence on the streets: "Oh as for those people who come to the market, they see us as a bunch of vagabonds and delinquent people. Sometimes the way they stare at you. They think we do not want to work, and we sleep outside, so they think of us as bad people and we are not part of the human race. That makes me feel sad because if I lived at home, these people will not have the opportunity to despise me."

Ekua goes further to state, when asked whether they will be arrested by law enforcement officials only in situations where anyone of them engaged in illegal activities, "No, unless there is a big fight to attract the police or someone causes some kind of trouble. If we stay out of trouble the police do not bother us at all." Ekua is hopeful that her goal of becoming a hair stylist will materialize. She states, "My wish is to find someone here who would volunteer to help me." Although no timetable has been set, Ekua believes going back home with or without any tangibles is the only option, but for now, all she has is hope and resilience that will propel the turbines as she pursues her dream. Ekua knows so well that returning home unsuccessful will bring unforgiving judgments on her. She said, "If I do not find anyone willing to help me, I will eventually return to my village. I know it would be difficult and my people will be unsympathetic, but if that is my fate, I am content with that." Ekua's account is one of many that this book seeks to detail as well as the push and pull factors involved in this migratory pattern within the Ghanaian context.

Chapter Two
The Known Contributors

Previous studies on this phenomenon in the Western world have applied the terms "runaway," "homeless," and "street youth" interchangeably, and rightfully so, because it is highly unlikely to find any one of these social categories existing independent of each other as presented by Cauce & Morgan (1994), Kurtz et al. (1991), Unger et al. (1998), and Whitbeck & Simons (1990). Some studies have attempted to connect these categories, that runaway behavior often spawns youth homelessness, which ultimately leads to the creation of street youth. The study of the etiology of runaway behavior in the Western world has been evaluated by several independent groups including Bender-Pari (1997), *Economist* (2002), Whitbeck & Hoyt (2001), Ek & Steelman (1988), Patterson-Taylor (2000), Teare & Peterson (1994), Tyler et al. (2000), and Yoder et al. (2001). These studies have demonstrated emotional and sometimes physical and sexual abuse as well as other forms of unnurturing family circumstances such as domestic abuse and mental health problems, mainly due to substance abuse, as some of the major factors underlying this pattern. These factors ultimately provide a clear distinction between the youth who leave home for the streets on voluntary basis and the "throwaways." The decision to roam the streets by the latter category, "throwaway" youth, is born of necessity (*Economist*, 2002; Patterson-Taylor, 2000). Although there are several other studies that clearly distinguish these categories, almost all these studies share one thing in common: the array of factors that trigger this phenomenon (Cauce & Morgan, 1994; Unger, Kipke et al., 1998; Cook & Birchman, 1997; Kryder-Coe et al., 1991; Kurtz et al., 1991; Tyler et al.,

2000; Whitbeck & Simons, 1990). Ultimately, these studies provide, to large extent, the motive for leaving home for the streets as anticipation of opportunities in whatever shape or form. It must be emphasized that the ability to fully establish the causes of this phenomenon provides a vital step in our march toward attaining a comprehensive, effective, affordable, and sustainable system of intervention.

Over the years, studies on the African situation have identified rural–urban migration as the main causal factor in establishing this social class (Beauchemin, 1999; Eloundou-Enyegue & Stokes, 2002; Shanahan, 2002). However, by failing to evaluate the role culture may play in the creation of this phenomenon (Mufume, 2000), there is the propensity to equate the African situation to that of the Western world, especially in the case of the "throwaways" where the decision to leave home for the street is driven almost exclusively by utter need. By so doing, some researchers in this field have attempted to elucidate this African situation using the Western family system as a surrogate tool.

Although earlier studies have shown a broad range of factors, which include economy, culture, and family, that trigger the emergence of children on urban streets in Africa, these studies placed emphasis only on the apparent differences between the Western world and Africa (Eloundou-Enyegue & Stokes, 2002; Mufume, 2000). Notwithstanding, these pioneering studies have provided the needed momentum in an effort to understand and mount a viable campaign against this crisis on the continent.

Studies by Beauchemin (1999) and Mufume (2000) demonstrated that economic restructuring, an attempt at initiating and sustaining meaningful economic changes in Africa, has had unintended casualties, one of them being increased homelessness among youth. An effort by international funding agencies to restructure African economies via programs such as the structural adjustment in an attempt to improve infrastructure and institute democracy ultimately led to massive retrenchment.

Parifait Eloundou-Enyegue and Shannon Stokes (2002) hypothesized that the economic and income gap between rural and urban communities coupled with a decline in fosterage has played a major role in the migration of youth from rural areas. Fosterage has, for a long time, played a role in the economic mobility of children from rural to urban families due to the ever-widening income and infrastructure gap between these communities.

Eloundou-Enyegue and Stokes (2002) have reported that a precipitous decline in fosterage is secondary to declining African economies. These authors also reported that a downward trajectory in urban fosterage opportunities since the 1980s has resulted in a dramatic increase in the population of street children, as is currently the case in many African urban communities.

It is worth noting that the nexus of the extended family system in Africa served as the economic and social unit within the rural community until the advent of modernization (Mufume, 2000). Modernization, through westernization (Little, 1957; Caldwell, 1968) continues to serve as a powerful magnet sweeping across the African continent, snatching sons and daughters of peasants from their rural homes and placing them in urban communities. The result is massive rural–urban migration that has severely impacted the very foundations of the extended family system, causing it to crumble at an alarming rate. In addition, unlike Western Europe, rather unfortunately, urbanization in Africa has and continues to grow out of proportion relative to industrialization, leaving a legion of rural youth chasing very few urban job opportunities. This situation has led to an irreversible collapse of the very role the extended family structure was established to play.

These findings suggest that an attempt to evaluate this crisis will require a detailed contextual understanding of the African cultural system, unlike that within the Western world. African researchers conclude that environmental factors play a more significant role in the emergence of street children on urban streets within the continent. The incessant decline in the already fragile African economies and the ever-widening income gap between the rural and urban communities catalyze and entrench these manifestations.

One African country that has attracted much attention in the last decade on this ever-growing crisis on the African continent is Ghana, located within the West African subregion. This street child phenomenon, until the 1990s, was relatively unknown to Ghana and academics in this area of research. A 1992 unpublished report by the University of Ghana had the number of street children in many parts of the Greater Accra Region at 4,000, most of whom were on the streets of the administrative capital, Accra. Another survey by Catholic Action for Street Children four years later recorded 10,401 street children within this region; and, by 2006, the number had risen to a staggering 21,143. The Ghana Government Department of Social Welfare—in collaboration with Ricerca e Cooperazione, an Italian international organization; Catholic Action for Street Children; and Street Girls Aid—has made higher projections for the years ahead. These figures paint a clear picture of the pace at which this phenomenon is growing and signal an even more gloomy future.

Currently, the presence of street children on urban streets in Ghana is palpable, and it is routine to find these children by the roadsides engaging in all kinds of menial services ranging from vending to carting of goods. Unfortunately, the reward for their hard work is disproportionately low, making the ascent to the summit even more difficult. Like other African countries, urbanization and consumerism in combination with factors such as parental neglect have contributed immensely to the influx of rural youth onto urban streets (Beauchemin, 1999). The allure is even more intense considering the fact that there is huge rural-urban income and infrastructure disparity across the country as reported by Assibey-Mensah (1998), Fentimen and Hall (1999), Shanahan (2002), and Quist (2001). This trend appears to show no sign of receding in recent years as the already-declining economy is faced with free-market policies, which tend to broaden the gap between rich and poor, thus entrenching rural poverty (Assimeng,

1999, p. 98; McCreery, 2001). It has become abundantly clear that migrant youths leave the rural communities with little or no realistic impression of how little the urban community has to offer and end up living on the streets in an attempt to stay afloat.

On the basis of the preceding discourse, it is evident that unlike the Western world, rural–urban migration is the cause of the influx of rural youth onto urban streets, which is systemic and entails declining economies and crushing poverty. One question that remains to be addressed is whether some variable or a set of variables apart from declining economies, the broad rural-urban income gap, poverty, or parental neglect exist to complete the puzzle. Why are these children not at all content with their placid rural life and are hell bent on leaving for the urban community by any means? For instance, over the years, the Ghanaian government has associated the problem of street children with inadequate parental supervision and hence takes a law enforcement approach to getting rid of them. One other approach some NGOs see as the way forward is simply to urge these children to return home. The real question is whether these and other intervention programs address the real problem or just have a placebo effect. Do these children have a story to tell those of us on the fringes, and will their story be one that will translate into a lasting solution or an effective compass to provide some guidance in our quest to formulating a solution that is sustainable? It must be emphasized that though previous studies have had to incorporate a discourse with these children at the center of the protocol, these are more often than not preformulated questionnaire questions that are posed to accept or reject a given hypothesis. What if these children were allowed to present their stories in an unlimited and spontaneous fashion that is completely free of some sort of mold? What is interesting is the fact that, although the initial lives of these children across the country are shaped by diverse sociocultural structures, these children end up having almost the same goal at one stage in their emotional and physical developmental process. Do these diverse rural social and cultural elements across the country have any role to play in the cause and/or sustenance of this phenomenon? These are very pertinent questions that cannot be ignored. It is therefore imperative to take a closer look at this dimension of the Ghanaian society and to evaluate the potential of this aspect to induce and/or facilitate this crisis and to what extent. To effectively address this question will require an emic approach based on the thoughts and experiences of these homeless children and their rural families. The incentive associated with this approach, the author believes, will provide a rare window of opportunity to further explore this phenomenon to the very core, and the only way forward to achieving this is establishing a direct and candid interaction with this cohort. Offering a curious, attentive, and objective ear to these children is considered a very vital step in our match towards attaining our cherished goal of limiting this crisis by understanding the problem and mounting the most effective intervention program(s) in an objective comprehensive and sustained fashion.

This book, by utilizing stories from Ghanaian street children without a preconceived structure and explaining the family circumstances through the application of theory, seeks to provide a broader understanding of the Ghanaian phenomenon. Given the broad public misconception and the minimal attention the Ghanaian situation attracts from the government, this volume aims at establishing a didactic discourse in the country, and it is my conviction that these findings as documented herein will provide a more profound understanding of the remote causal factors and provide a platform for effective communication as well as facilitation of existing intervention programs.

Chapter Three
Scope of the Study

This study was conducted in the Northern and Greater Accra regions of Ghana over a seven-year period and utilized a phenomenological approach where the participants were allowed to narrate and interpret their own experiences. A qualitative approach was utilized in this study because it allowed for a more effective and objective evaluation of real life experiences (Byrne, 2001). The advantage here is to be able to illuminate the Ghanaian phenomenon through the participants' own perceptions and experiences and not the researcher's interpretation of the situation or by extrapolation from street child phenomena. The author is of the opinion that this method will provide the means to uncover emerging meanings from the perspective of the research participants through interviews, discussions, and field observations. A section of this chapter provides a brief description of the country and the regions within which the study was conducted.

Ghana is a country located off the Gulf of Guinea, about eight degrees north of the Equator, and spans an area of 238,500 km^2 (92,085 mi^2) (Extreme points.com, 2010). It is bordered by the Republic of Togo to the east, Côte d'Ivoire to the west, and Burkina Faso to the north, all francophone nations. The country's topography is characterized by flat plains, low hills, and rivers, the major being the Volta River, which extends through large portions of eastern Ghana with the Oti and Afram rivers as its affluents. The coastline is mostly a low, sandy shore backed by plains and scrub and intersected by several rivers and streams, while the northern part of the country features high plains.

Southwest and south-central Ghana is made up of a forested plateau region consisting of the Ashanti uplands, the Kwahu Plateau, and the hilly Akuapim-Togo Ranges along the country's eastern border. The Volta Basin also takes up most of central Ghana with the country's highest point being Mount Afadjato (885 m, 2,904 ft) in the Akwapim-Togo Ranges. The eastern coastal belt is warm and comparatively dry; the southwest corner, warm and humid; and the northern belt tends to be warm with relatively low humidity around the year.

Ghana's human population is approximately twenty-four million with broad demographics. In fact Ghana is home to several ethnic groups, with English as the official language after British colonial rule. The ethnic groups are the Akan (which includes the Fante, Akyem, Ashanti, Kwahu, Akuapem, Nzema, Bono, Akwamu, Ahanta, and others) accounting for 49 percent; Mole-Dagbon, 15 percent; Ewe, 12 percent; Ga-Dangme (comprising of the Ga, Adangbe, Ada, Krobo, and others), 7 percent; Guan, 4 percent; Gurma, 4 percent; Gurunsi, 3 percent; Mande-Busanga, 1 percent; Hausa, Zabarema, and Fulani, 1.8 percent; and other tribes, 1.4 percent (2000 census) (CIA World Factbook, 2010). Religious sects include Christianity, 68.8 percent; Islam, 15.9 percent; and Traditional African religion, 8.5 percent (International Religious Freedoms Report, 2007).

Although well endowed with natural resources, Ghana remains somewhat dependent mainly on trade and international assistance. About 28 percent of the population lives below the international poverty line of US$1.25 a day, the vast majority of which are Ghanaian women from the politically marginalized and poor northern and upper regions of the country (CNN, 2009), and according to the World Bank, Ghana's per capita income has barely doubled over the past forty-five years. Ghana, known for its gold in colonial times, still remains one of the world's top gold producers with other exports such as cocoa, timber, electricity, diamond, bauxite (Aluworks Limited, 2010), and manganese as sources of foreign exchange. Ongoing oil exploration is expected to provide a tremendous inflow of capital into the economy (Rigzone.com, 2010). The Akosombo Dam, constructed on the Volta River, serves as the main source of electrical power for the country and its neighboring countries. Ghana's labor force in 2008 totaled about 11.5 million people (CIA World Factbook, 2010). The economy continues to rely heavily on subsistence agriculture, which accounts for about 37 percent of the gross domestic product (GDP) and provides employment for 56 percent of the work force (CIA World Factbook, 2010), mainly small landholders. Manufacturing forms a small fraction of the Ghanaian economy, accounting for 7.9 percent of the GDP as of 2007.

In the 1960s, the urban population of Ghana totaled 1,551,174 persons, representing 23.1 percent of the country's total population. By 1970, this had risen to 28 percent. This number rose to 32 percent in 1984 and was estimated to increase by a percentage point by 1992. The rate of urbanization varies among the ten administrative regions. While the Greater Accra Region showed an 83 percent urban residency, the Ashanti Region matched the national average of 32 percent as of 1984. In the same year, the Upper West Region of the country recorded only 10 percent of its population residing in urban communities, which is reflective of the asymmetry between the northern and southern belts, with the latter holding the lion's share of the minerals and forest resources within the country.

The process of urbanization in Ghana, like that of much of the continent of Africa, predates the arrival of Europeans and colonization (Dickson, 1971; Anderson & Rathbone, 2000) and was on a "pilot scale" during this precolonization era. The spurt of urbanization was observed during the European colonization and the introduction of the Western economic system with its market economy (Little, 1974; Owusu, 2005a). The colonial and postcolonial investment strategies established basic criteria of investing in regions based on the level of exploitable and exportable resources, which became a good determinant of the distribution profile of basic infrastructure. This pattern of infrastructure allocation acted as the major factor that determined the population dynamics, with areas rich in exploitable and exportable resources recording higher population growth and development relative to other regions of the country (Konadu-Agyemang & Adanu, 2003).

For instance, communities within the southern belt of the country enjoy climatic conditions well suited for the cultivation of cash crops and are endowed with forest resources, such as lumber and spices, as well as mineral resources, namely, gold, diamonds, and bauxite. By default, facilities such as refineries and ports in the middle belt and coastal regions were established to support these investments (Dickson, 1971, 1975), with northern Ghana geographically disadvantaged and firmly entrenched in the basement in terms of these investments. Hence, this kind of distribution profile of investments placed the southern regions well ahead of the northern territories in terms of infrastructural and socioeconomic development. More significantly, this pattern of economic activities became a major factor in determining population dynamics and, to a large extent, enhanced urban concentration as existing and new centers emerged as collecting points for locally produced exportable commodities, as well as administrative and communication centers. In addition, the fact that marine transportation was the main trade route between continents during the precolonial years placed European settlers on the coastal areas, leading to a reorientation of trade routes. Thus, the southern territories enjoyed direct access, and the northern territories, due to their land-locked status, were geographically disadvantaged. It must be emphasized that there was some level of modest economic activity thanks to the trans-Saharan trade between the northern territories of the West African countries including Ghana and the Islamicized states in North Africa. However, these activities declined with the introduction of European travel to the West African coast, as was case when the Portuguese journeys around the West African coast opened up new trade avenues between Europe and West Africa. By the early sixteenth century, European trading bases, the "factories" established on the Atlantic coast, and trade with the wealthier Europeans assured the prime importance of West Africa versus the trade activities in the north. One other strike against the trans-Saharan trade was the fact that North Africa had declined in both political and economic importance, while the Saharan crossing remained long and treacherous. In all likelihood, the blow that put an end to this trade activity in the north was the year-long battle of Tondibi in 1591–1592, when Morocco crossed the Sahara and launched an attack on Timbuktu, Gao, and some other centers that were crucial to the trade. This disruption to trade led to a dramatic decline in the importance of these cities and resulted in a precipitous reduction in trade activities.

It must be emphasized that while the economic activities within the southern sector of the country were the broad forces that intensified the process of urbanization in these regions, the process itself, as in many other parts of Africa, was characterized by the fact that there were few urban centers that could accommodate the expanding population. This trend raised a lot of attention within the circles of development planning because it was considered to negatively impact spatial economy within country.

On the basis of this, an array of planning strategies were implemented with the primary objective of minimizing this population polarization and producing a more balanced settlement pattern. Prominent among these strategies, the growth pole concept and the Integrated Rural Development Program were designed to stimulate rural development to curtail out-migration from the rural communities (Thomi & Yankson, 1985). The growth pole concept was aimed at ensuring that development impulses were transmitted throughout a whole economy through poles or centers of attraction from which economic activities are generated throughout a specifically defined regional space. These included urban communities, industry, and infrastructure such as airports, tourist centers, or tertiary education institutions, many of which were put in place to advance economic development throughout their environs as a trickle-down type of socioeconomic development. In fact, it is a basic requirement for a growth pole strategy that developmental impulses (the potential of which should be exploited to the highest level possible) occur in several places within the country or at least be the focus under a planned development program. Therefore, growth poles were identified in depressed and underdeveloped areas, making use of existing economic potentials of the communities.

Unfortunately, over the years, these strategies have failed to reverse the trend of urbanization and settlement within the countries. In recent years, attempts at transforming the settlement hierarchy or at least slowing down the growth rate of the urban communities have centered on decentralization and the promotion of small towns and rural development (Owusu, 2004, 2005b), which will be discussed in the subsequent section. Though the small town development strategy is not a novel concept, what is innovative here is the association of this concept with a decentralization program. The increasing transfer of resources and administrative and legal authority to the district level under the country's decentralization program was expected to enhance district-level development and, in particular, promote district capitals as attractive centers to curb the rate of influx of migrants to the existing urban center (GSS, 1995; Owusu, 2004; Owusu & Lund, 2004; Owusu, 2005b).

Although several years have passed since the inception of this program, the tide of the urbanization process has failed to deliver the expected outcome in terms of population dynamics. For instance, formal census data indicates a dramatic increase in Ghana's population, especially within the urban centers since the 1920s. In fact, it has been reported that the increase in concentration of the population in settlements of five thousand or more people constitutes the greatest fraction of the overall population of the country (Andræ, 1981; Thomi & Yankson, 1985; GSS, 1995; Yeboah & Waters, 1997). The proportion of the total Ghanaian population representing urban residents increased tremendously from 7.8 percent in 1921 to 23.1 percent by 1960, and by the year 2000, the value had risen to a staggering 43.8 percent (GSS, 2002a).

Urban areas in Ghana have customarily enjoyed better infrastructure compared with rural locations, but, again, this pattern disproportionately favors the south. Consequently, Kumasi, Accra, and many towns within the southern economic belt tend to attract more rural folk than the dry, underdeveloped savanna regions of the north. The extension of the national electricity grid to the northern sector in the late 1980s may have helped in stabilizing the north-south flow, but to a very modest extent. Notwithstanding the rate of growth of urban population, Ghana continues to be a nation of rural communities. The 1984 enumeration showed that six of the country's ten regions had rural populations of 5 percent or more above the national average of 68 percent. Rural residency was estimated to be 67 percent of the population in 1992. These figures, though reflecting a trend toward urban residency, were comparable to those recorded in the 1970s, where about 72 percent of the nation's population lived in rural communities.

The Greater Accra Region

Geographically, the Greater Accra Region accounts for approximately 1.4 percent of the total land mass of the country with a population of 2,905,726 as of the year 2000, accounting for about 15 percent of the country's total population, making this region the most densely populated since the 1960s. The population density has increased from 167 per km^2 at that time to 441 in 1984, and to 896 per km^2 by the year 2000. The growth rate of 4.4 percent between 1984 and 2000 far exceeds the national average of 2.7 percent per annum, indicating a doubling time of sixteen years. The corresponding increase of persons aged fifteen to sixty-four has been attributed in part to the influx of migrants in search of job opportunities in industrialized urban Accra and metropolitan hubs of the region. For instance, the Accra and metropolitan district has the largest population, standing at approximately 57 percent with a high concentration of street children. More recently, youths have migrated from all rural areas of the country to the more urbanized regions, with the Greater Accra Region experiencing the highest influx (Beauchemin, 1999).

Unlike the Northern Region, a typical household within the Greater Accra Region accommodates between five and seven family members. Due to the tradition of the extended family system, most households will have the component of other relatives with the members of the nuclear family. The proportion of grandchildren within a household could range between 11 and 13 percent, indicating that couples are likely to live with their parents or parents-in-law.

Greater than 75 percent of households in the region has access to electrical power, again a clear indication of the level of development of this region versus that of the northern belt. The alternative source of energy is kerosene, which is mostly utilized in the more rural districts. Although this region, especially the Accra and Tema metropolitan areas, enjoys an adequate supply of electricity, about 59 percent utilize charcoal as the main source of energy for cooking, with electrical power supplying electrical bulbs and other installations. About 22 percent of households in the region, a fourfold increase compared with the Northern Region, use liquefied petroleum gas for cooking, which can be attributed to the proximity of this region to the refineries and the relatively greater income level within this region.

Approximately 50 percent of the population, fifteen years and older, is married either by law or in consensual union. In spite of the minimum legal age of eighteen years, there are some reports that girls aged between twelve and seventeen years do get married to older males analogous to the Northern Region and accounting for about 1.7 percent, compared with the national average of 6.4 percent.

About 77 to 85 percent of the region is literate, which is far greater than the national average of 38 percent, an indication of the skewed literacy rate across the country. About 30 to 40 percent of the population receives middle school education, 9 to 18 percent high school, and 3 to 6 percent tertiary education.

The region has an unemployment rate of about 13.4 percent, greater than the national average of 10.4 percent. About 8 percent of the economically active population is engaged in agriculture, forestry, fishing, and hunting. Contrary to expectation, fishing is not the main industry, although the Atlantic Ocean lies next door to the south. The private informal sector (commerce and manufacturing) accounts for about 60 percent of the economically active population. These are usually sole proprietors or sole traders who own and run the business; and there is absolutely no legal distinction between the owner and the establishment. Females appear to dominate the private informal sector, with the vast proportion of the male population engaging in the public and private formal sectors, a clear evidence of gender disparity. Although the literacy rate appears to be relatively high, the private formal sector takes up about 23 percent and the public sector, 12 percent.

Although the economically active population is fifteen years and older, the 2000 Population and Housing Census showed the existence of a class of working children in this region and around the country engaged in family enterprises (Ghana Statistical Service, 2003), a practice proscribed by the Children's Act of 1998, which prohibits individuals less than thirteen years of age from engaging in any kind of activity for purely financial reasons. In fact, the numbers indicate that about 10 percent of the population of children ranging from seven to fourteen years is economically active, with almost equal gender distribution in this cohort across the region.

The Northern Region

The Northern Region is the largest of the ten regions of Ghana in terms of land mass, with a population of approximately 1,820,806, representing 9.6 percent of the country's population. The region is, linguistically and culturally, more diverse than the politically and economically dominant regions of central and southern Ghana. The Northern Region is one of the least developed in terms of infrastructure and commerce, and has for many years been the source of migrating youths (Piel, 1968). The culturally diverse nature of the region has led to more frequent conflicts within the area, further limiting development and increasing poverty.

The average household in the region holds approximately ten members compared to the national average of nine, a clear indication of overcrowding. Children constitute on the average 45 percent of each household; 22 percent are external family. This situation exerts pressure on the household resources such as water, toilet facilities, and food. The quality of housing is generally below average across the region. Most of the homes are constructed from mud with thatch for roofing. Most dwelling units have no electricity, running water, or modern and improved toilet facilities.

About 77 percent of households use kerosene lamps as the source of lighting, while 22 percent of residents within the Tamale municipality, the regional capital, has access to electricity power. About 84 percent of households in the region utilize wood as the main source of energy for cooking, and women are often tasked to gather firewood from the surrounding vegetation. Charcoal is used by 12 percent and a paltry 5 percent can afford alternative forms of energy, such as electricity and liquefied petroleum gas, for cooking purposes.

Greater than 50 percent of the population within the region is married either by law or in consensual union. The divorce rate is low, less than 10 percent, and is comparable to the fraction that is widowed. Less than 0.5 percent of the population aged 12 to 14 years is married. In some cases these girls are married into polygamous homes. Those in consensual union, separated, divorced, and widowed each accounts for less than 1 percent. The fact that there are twelve- to fourteen-year-olds already divorced or widowed may be due to very young girls being married to much older men, who either divorce them or pass away early in the relationship.

About 22 percent of the population, fifteen years and older, is literate compared with the national level of 38 percent. Mainly this is due to a lack of schools and minimal accessibility to those that exist. Approximately 48 percent of the population acquire grade school education; with 22 percent going on to enroll in middle school, 13 percent in high school, and only 5 percent in vocational institutions. Tertiary education is attained by 10 percent. In all these categories, except at grade school level, greater male enrollment is recorded. This holds true for most of the districts in that it is routine to see the males provide labor on the farms at that age.

Subsistence agriculture and fishing are the main economic activities within the region with agriculture accounting for about 71 percent of the economically active population, and the private informal and formal sectors constituting less than 5 percent. The rural areas constitute the focus of agriculture and fishing, with limited activity in the Tamale municipality. This situation is a result of the fact that the region is unable to attract human resource and capital due to the unfavorable climate and the potential for conflict among the tribes.

In an attempt to curb the consequent socioeconomic impact on urban growth, the "Rural Manifesto," which was crafted to evaluate the causes of rural underdevelopment, was introduced in April 1984. Under this manifesto, some development strategies were evaluated and implemented to make rural residency more appealing. In pursuit of this, two basic steps were taken: the establishment by the Bank of Ghana of more than 120 rural banks across the country to serve as local credit facilities for rural entrepreneurs, and the rural electrification program initiated in the late 1980s. As part of the package, the government established district assemblies as a component of its strategy for rural improvement through decentralized administration, a program designed to afford the rural communities governance at their doorstep and greater involvement in planning and executing development programs within their communities.

Ghana's Decentralization and Local Government Program

In 1988, aside from institution-sponsored adjustments, the government of Ghana embarked on the decentralization of administration by putting in place a program to facilitate a greater degree of local autonomy as a pathway to enhancing the efficiency of the various district administrations necessary to local development, which by default hinged on the infrastructural needs of the rural community. To a greater extent, this devolutionary model was sponsored by the government to bring structural adjustment reform to the doorstep of the local communities. The objective was to promote effective and accountable local government comprising the highest political, administrative, planning, development, budgeting, and rating authorities, collectively called a District Assembly or Local Government.

Among the array of objectives under this program, rural development appeared to be the central goal of the District Assemblies as a means of reducing out-migration to the urban communities and actually redirecting population movement from highly populated urban areas with little industrial potential to other areas that previously were unattractive in terms of basic infrastructure but had the potential to provide lucrative agricultural job opportunities (GSS, 1995, pp. 12–14; Ayee, 1997, p. 38). Under this program, the District Assemblies or Local Governments, a term a section of the public chose to use, were established across the country and handled additional socioeconomic, political, and legal responsibilities ranging from environmental conservation to provision of social services. The implementation of this program led to the promulgation of the Provisional National Defense Council Law 207, giving legal backing to the creation of District Assemblies and the establishment of 110 districts in the country. As a result, the District Assemblies were assigned the task, with a broad range of functions that empowered them to provide decentralized and devolved local public services to the people. Although these institutions signaled the willingness of the central government to bring power to the doorstep of the local community, it was apparent that very little power had dissipated and the central administration enjoyed total control in some key aspects of this model, such as:

- All by-laws must be approved by the minister of local government and rural development.
- The president has the power to unilaterally dissolve defaulting or nonperforming district assemblies, thereby ignoring the role of the electorate.
- The minister of local government and rural development reserves the power to issue guidelines as they relate to acquisition of licenses and permits or rates levied by District Assemblies.
- The provision of Section 88 of the Local Government Act, Act 462, required that the District Assemblies seek approval of the central government to modulate loans offered to local entrepreneurship. This instance gave credence to how much power the central government wielded and the tenacity with which the central authority held on to it.

This program led to the direct replacement of the existing 65 district councils established and operated since the mid-1970s. With the social, economic, political, and legal roles clearly defined, coupled with the appropriate political and legal backing, these assemblies had in their custody the political, administrative, and development mandate necessary for these institutions to pursue their aspirations (GSS, 2008).

The establishment of additional districts meant that new district capitals had to be established and assigned, a step that provided the recipe for infrastructural and economic advancement. Assigning an administrative status to these local communities was, in itself, enough to attract public infrastructure and promote an influx of population, eventually transforming these communities into towns. One additional benefit from this decentralization program was the fact that several government, NGO, and other donor agency initiatives provided the needed support for participatory democratic development in these communities. These institutions provided the legal and logistical instruments in these communities, particularly the district capitals or administrative centers, to enable them to perform their new role more effectively, as it became clear that these local administrative units were faced with an array of challenges. This support was absolutely necessary considering the fact that most local communities were pristine and had never experienced any infrastructural or economic growth, coupled with the fact that the very low literacy rate in these areas unfortunately rendered the process even more daunting. Some of the programs and projects that were designed specifically for the target district capitals were the District Assemblies Common Fund, a constitutional provision that allocates 5 percent of the total national revenue to District Assemblies; the World Bank and United Nations Development Program's Urban V projects, targeting roads and sanitation problems; European Union microproject schemes; and the German Agency for Technical Assistance/Ghana Government (Ministry of Local Government and Rural Development) project titled "Promotion of District Capitals". The policy of the central government and the Ministry of Local Government and Rural Development was to provide each district capital with accessible road links, connect these communities to the national electricity grid, establish a functional communication system, and provide sustainable district health facilities, accessible and affordable clean drinking water, and basic education at the secondary/technical school levels (GSS, 1995; Owusu, 2004, 2005b). These were measures the government believed constituted the basic requirements for a socioeconomic takeoff. These improvements and increased transfer of resources to these communities have marginally contributed to the economic and infrastructural growth of district capitals and other settlements within the districts (GSS, 1995; Acheampong, 1996).

The marginal impact of the decentralization program in terms of growth is generally attributed to the very primordial status of the District Assemblies prior to the implementation of the program and the tide of numerous bottlenecks working against this model. This negative obviously accounts for the continuous concentration of the population in a few urban centers (GSS, 2002a, pp. 2–3;

Ghana Poverty Reduction Strategy [GPRS], 2002, p. 16), and thus the fundamental program's objective of improving the socioeconomic status of the local people within these districts and facilitating the geographical flow of development to these communities as a means of curbing rural–urban migration has yet to fully materialize. The disproportionate distribution of national resources and development was a negative that piled on the haystack within which the needle was located.

A study conducted by Razin and Obirih-Yeboah concluded that local governments in the administrative capital (Accra-Tema District Assembly) and in the second-largest metropolitan area, Kumasi in the Ashanti Region, and other large urban centers attracted the most financial support, compared to the remote and predominantly rural local communities (2000). Financial allocations from the central government, such as the District Assemblies' Common Fund, were found to favor the large urban centers. In a way, this is to be expected in that these metropolitan communities exhibit a higher rate of population increase relative to their rural counterparts due to out-migration from the rural regions. In addition, fiscally advantaged urban communities enjoy relatively higher self-generated revenue as they have a broader tax base. This allows these assemblies to enjoy some level of autonomy and implement more development programs with relatively lower fiscal support from the central government, which routinely come with stringent guidelines and in most cases have little or no reference to local circumstances. So along with the problems associated with the inability of the other District Assemblies to generate revenue independent of the central government transfers, the findings by Razin and Obirih-Yeboah and other studies have demonstrated that even though decentralization has to a large extent improved the level of flow of resources from the central government to these local districts that hitherto had minimal or no fiscal backing from the central government, the dynamics of this model have failed to provide equity in the redistribution of resources and economic growth among these remote and desolate communities (Ayee, 1995; Asibuo, 2000).

Lastly, the existence of limited employment opportunities within these remote regions and continuous out-migration to the metropolitan communities over the years is a measure of how marginal the decentralization performance in the rural communities and other small towns has been. This situation exists because these areas are directly affected by the very forces, such as the abject lack of basic infrastructure, which hinder job creation in large towns/cities. This is to be expected as these communities have been and are still in the negative on the development scale.

A rural household study was conducted in eight local communities of two districts, Dunkwa-on-Offin and Twifo Praso, within the remote areas of the Central Region. The flexibility of the give-and-take interview format with individual households allowed the researchers to get an in-depth understanding of how the decentralization program impacted the rural-urban linkages. The study revealed that although a substantial proportion, representing approximately 61 percent of the respondents, has no intention of relocating, the rest indicated it was a good idea to relocate to the metropolitan communities, especially to the Accra-Tema, Kumasi, and Sekondi-Takoradi urban centers. An overwhelming majority of the respondents cited the lack of jobs and employment opportunities as the major contributory factor underlying the unattractive nature of these regions of the country.

Chapter Four

Poverty in Africa: The Role of the United Nations

Although sub-Saharan Africa is plagued with disease such as HIV/AIDS, rising infant mortality, high population growth, and the incidence of war, the steep decline in per capita income due to marginal GDP growth has become synonymous with these countries over the years.

The United Nations' assessment of the African socioeconomic crisis, which became a hot issue in the 1970s, identified drought and famine in the 1980s as key factors. Drought in Southern Africa; ravaging war in some spots on the continent; the rate of urbanization outpacing industrialization; the rising incidence of infant mortality, due especially to substandard health facilities; the threat of child-killer diseases; high population growth; illiteracy; mass unemployment; and limited essential public services have triggered and sustained mass poverty (UN, 1987).

With the ever-declining socioeconomic well-being of most of these countries, especially those within the sub-Saharan region of the continent, it appears the United Nations-sponsored program has not been able to fulfill the socioeconomic needs of the populations. For example, African strategic planning, demonstrated through the Lagos Plan of Action and the United Nations Program of Action for Economic Recovery and Development 1986–1990, emphasized strategies that focus attention on major social issues, the development of human resources, and the needs of special population groups, particularly women and youth (UN, 1987, p. 3). It is within this context that the current and future role of social provisions must be given the necessary consideration by reinforcing this component of policy. For instance, the Lagos Plan of Action states:

> The primary objective of socio-economic development lies with the improvement of the economic and social well being of the entire populations of these countries within the sub-region. To fulfill this benchmark requires the complete participation of all segments of the population in viable and productive economic ventures as well as the provision of all the basic social and commercial apparatus directed at improving the socio-economic needs of the entire community. (UN, 1987, p. 3)

In theory, this alliance between the strategic plans and the objectives of social work practice appeared to have a perfect set of attributes, but there is compelling evidence that these strategies were plagued with complex problems at the implementation stage, and so it comes as no surprise that only modest gains were achieved. In 1987, the United Nations recommended that policy must be formulated with the mass of the population, especially those who live in rural communities, as the target segment of the community, as related to the reorganization and reinforcing of the urban informal sector as well as the rebuilding and refocusing of the capacities of social institutions, policies, and programs. Experts believed these propositions required the infusion of historical, sociopolitical, and economic experience realities as well as the cultural heritage of member countries. It is only when these requirements are met that the adjustment program will make significant strides toward achieving a more friendly socioeconomic climate.

A section of the community is of the opinion that social considerations constitute a critical ingredient for achieving the desired socioeconomic goals. This then implies that social work has a central role to play in this effort (Osei-Hwedie, 1990), and that means ridding the system of foreign perceptions and perhaps redefining its central focus, knowledge, and value base (Mupedziswa, 1992; Taback, 1991; Midgley, 1990, 1981; Khinduka, 1971), a fundamental requirement without which, these pundits believe, any meaningful progress cannot be achieved in this direction. It must be noted that all these propositions constituted internal maneuvers that yielded marginal changes.

In fact, stunted economic growth in these countries in the last three decades has severely impacted these once middle-income countries just like some of the south Asian countries, transforming them into low-income countries with an average per capita GDP growth below 1 percent and, in some cases, in the negative. Some Western experts have offered their own version as it relates to the factors they believe serve as triggers and driving forces that sustain the economic nonperformance associated with these countries. Some of these factors include the poor economic and political stewardship on the part of these governments coupled with inadequate social capital (Collier & Gunning, 1999). The proposition that this unhealthy economic climate across the subregion is a direct consequence of poor governance is rooted in the fact that most of these administrations were typically undemocratic, with the educated and urban residents, who in most cases have very little or no agricultural or commercial interests, comfortably occupying the driver's seat.

Additionally, the urban community, which serves as the political base of these individual administrations, pushed legislation for tax increases on agriculture, which forms the largest employment base for rural inhabitants, with a disproportionately low financial and logistic support for public agronomic research. With this policy in place, exports, which had and continue to have agriculture as one of the vital components of the engine that drives foreign exchange, inevitably took a hit with a decline in GDP and a balance of payments as the obvious manifestations. As stifling as the socioeconomic climate in these sub-Saharan countries and those in other regions around the world are, with minimal export capability and a consequent quick decline in GDP, these countries had no option, at least not in the short term, but to go for the lifeline, from any system or organization that was willing to extend it. The Bretton Woods

Institutions—which is composed of the International Monetary Fund (IMF) and the World Bank and managed by some of the industrialized countries, with the major players being the United States and other economic giants such as England and, to a lower extent, Japan---were quick to offer the financial "support" that was thought to be necessary to reverse the unfavorable balance of payments crises. With this offer, a fiscal association was born, and with it came the risk of losing complete control over domestic economic policies as they relate to macroeconomics, investment projects, and social spending in an effort to stabilize the unfavorable economic situation, although these countries are politically autonomous. This economic takeover, so to speak, by these multinational conglomerates of expatriate "experts" based in Washington, DC, took the form of a set of economic policies, which Williamson (1989) refers to as the "Washington consensus," that these ailing economies had no option, at least not in the short term, but to embrace and implement. This set of policies, inspired by these donor organizations, the so-called Structural Adjustment Programs, became economic tenets that these countries adhered to in a religious fashion, as long as they continued to receive financial bailout from these institutions.

We will take an in-depth look at the adjustment policies that are spelled out by these programs in subsequent sections of this book, with special reference to the two major donor institutions, the IMF and the World Bank, as well as delineate the package they claim offers the panacea for these ailing Third World economies and the responses arising in economies during or following the application of this socioeconomic "fix." But before we launch into this discussion, let us take a look at some of the theories that have been put forward by some experts, in an attempt to identify the causal factors underlying the debt crisis in Africa and other parts of the developing world.

Debt and Economic Crisis in Africa: A Theoretical Discourse

This section will discuss the debt crisis in developing countries within the continent of Africa using Nigeria as an example and consider some theories that offer possible explanations of this situation. Nigeria is one of the world's major oil-exporting countries, and it is expected that there will be more wealth in this country relative to the other countries in the West African subregion. However, there is mounting evidence of mass poverty across these countries, which is spreading very fast, with no respite in sight, at least not in the near future.

Various scholars in this field have offered different theories, in an attempt to make determinations as to the incidence and sustenance of decades of insolvency and of the extreme poverty situations that are now synonymous with these countries within the subcontinent. This never-ending debt and poverty crisis in these countries has ignited research projects that are aimed at providing some insight into the triggers of this stifling situation and explaining the complexities associated with this socioeconomic depression.

Different schools of thought have been put forward by various scholars in this discourse, and a section of the academic experts are of the opinion that the "dependency theory" (Baran, 1957; Frank, 1971) is well positioned to provide us with a high-definition snapshot of the causes underlying this monstrous socioeconomic crisis. Critics not only question the theme of the "dependency theory" but propose an alternative theory, the "development theory," which they believe offers a more compelling argument. The "development theory" proposed by Rostow, (1960) or "economic explanations" (Offiong, 1980), examines the socioeconomic needs along the lines of underdevelopment and development and offers strategies that the proponent believes will provide much-needed answers to this crisis. Last, but not the least, comes the "political explanations" (Migdal, 1988) or the "liberal theory" (Burchill, 1996). We will now discuss these theories in greater detail.

The Development Theory

This theory, as proposed by Rostow, examines the socioeconomic phenomena of "underdevelopment" and "development" and further analyzes as well as provides strategies aimed at achieving developmental goals in these fragile economies. This theory, which was put forth in the 1970s, has since undergone modification that conducts an assessment on the frequency at which a given society undergoes economic and developmental transformation (Smith, 2003). Rostow's theory contends that the sequence of economic steps toward modernization can be identified within a given society and include the following. The "traditional society," where the economy is stationary and dominated by traditional agricultural practices, is in part consistent with most areas of the sub-Saharan region where rural agricultural activities provide the bulk of food and other crops for foreign markets. The second stage, which Rostow referred to as the "preconditions for take-off" is the stage at which the rate of investments is on the rise, which then triggers a dynamic process of economic development, representing a manifestation of a nascent industrial revolution. In fact Ghana was selected as one of the countries for the United Nations Industrial Development Organization Integrated Program in 1998, soon after the introduction of this concept. This is one of a group of related programs currently in place or being pursued by the government of Ghana. The Ministry of Trade and Industry played a fundamental role in the design and preparation of this program in the country with the identification of specific areas for technical assistance as one of the series of steps toward its implementation.

The subsequent installation of a new administration in the year 2000 introduced some modifications in the program, which included activities considered to be of high priority, such as the expansion of the existing textile/garment training center, provision of an agricultural machinery industrial system, trade facilitation, creation of a technology innovation center for capital goods, and, finally, development of rural energy systems for off-grid villages. The third stage, the "take-off stage," entails full-blown dynamic economic growth within the system, a process that requires no external input, which is then followed by the "drive to maturity" stage, at which continual investments ranging from 40 to 60 percent are dominated by economic and technical advancements. This process of growth then culminates in the "age of high mass consumption," which is characterized by socioeconomic prosperity and several options in terms of goods and services. Considering the current socioeconomic situation in most of these countries in the subregion, the last two stages of Rostow's theory appear to be dreams for these countries, at least for now and in the near future.

It must be emphasized that what economic stages theories like Rostow's model seek to communicate to the broader audience is that specific criteria distinguish the stages of modernity from each other within the context of economic and social history of the community. Generally, "modernization" characterizes a rational conformity to the present or future requirements (Giddens, 1991). Giddens showed that a modern society is characterized by time-space distantiation and disembedding mechanisms, that a traditional society is based on direct interaction between people living close to each other, whereas modern societies stretch further and further across space and time using mass and interactive media. In this context, modernization appears to be the opposite of traditionalism, which seeks to maintain already existing customs and values of a given community. In fact, many consider traditionalism as conservative and "modernism" as the appearance of forms of social life or organization that emerged in Europe from about the seventeenth century and beyond (Giddens, 1991).

In this context, development, which means economic advancement, and underdevelopment, with obvious signs of poverty, are considered effects of dualism between traditional economic and social structures. In other words, underdevelopment appears to be the result of endogenous or internal factors, which means "development" is only possible by external factors that can be achieved only if there is a process of social, political-institutional, cultural, and technological "modernization" transformation. Within the industrialized world, economic and social modernization is based mainly on the platform of industrialization and democratization (Smith, 2003).

Interestingly, modernization theories tend to extrapolate Western development experiences to developing countries. It therefore comes as no surprise that industrialized countries in the Western world recommend that modernization efforts in the developing world use their experience as a blueprint, which, they believe, is the pathway that guarantees the transformation of the current socioeconomic status in these developing regions to at least middle-income level. This formula tends to put Rostow's theory in the category of a top-down approach, drawing a parallel between this proposition and the capitalist-oriented development scheme whereby development will have to trickle down from the urban-industrialized core to the periphery—in this case, from the developed to the developing countries (Stohr & Taylor, 1981; Potter, Binns, Elliot, & Smith, 1999). In effect, "development" in this context requires the evolutionary transition from a "premodern" or "traditional" to a "modern" society. Based on Rostow's proposition, the Dependency and Liberal economic theories represent an alternative wave of propositions.

The Dependency Theory

Proponents of the dependency theory contend that the debt crisis in Africa is the result of the extreme dependence of economies in Africa, especially those in the sub-Saharan region of the continent, on external financial bailout, which comes with competitive economic conditions over which these countries continue to have little or no control. The dependency theory is predicated on the notion that there is a "center" or "core" of wealthy industrialized countries in the Western world, and at the "periphery" occur the economically handicapped, underdeveloped countries. This theory goes further to suggest that resources move from the periphery (developing countries) toward the countries at the center or core, in this case, the developed world necessary to sustain their economic growth and wealth. The major contention here is that the economic development of these peripheral countries was rendered impossible by the domination of industrialized capitalist powers within the global economy (Offiong, 1980).

On the basis of this, proponents of this theory believe that the crushing poverty and mounting debt in these peripheral regions is attributed to the manner in which they integrate into the world economic system. The historical incorporation of dependent territories into the global division of labor may have led to this economic stagnation that is synonymous with these colonies and neocolonies (Sandbrook, 1982). There is concordance among a group of experts that the mammoth investments in these peripheral countries that are owned by United States–based conglomerates cannot be attributed to the capital transferred by these organizations out of the United States or other capital reserves in the Western world. This asymmetrical situation, as claimed by these scholars, is highlighted by the reported massive net returns of foreign exchange to the United States and other regions in the Western hemisphere, which appear to be growing at a startling pace and promising to linger for a long time to come. These scholars go further to assert that the economic success achieved by these conglomerates is inversely related to the socioeconomic well-being of these countries, which serve as the cradle of the very resources these organizations constantly mine with insatiable appetites. These peripheral countries, beset with poverty and ever-declining socioeconomic status, have no option but to turn to these institutions, which these countries believe have the magic touch for economic resurrection, and waste no time in accepting, with both hands, whatever package is given them. However, these grants and loans, once acquired, are swept away by a worsening balance of trade as fast as they came (Baran, 1954; Frank, 1971; Rodney, 1974). With time, these countries become addicted to external loans in anticipation that this strategy would eventually lead them out of the consuming economic crisis. Unfortunately, the donor organizations are always ahead of these struggling economies, and the terms under which these loans are granted tend to assume the "Trojan horse" scenario, with even more distressing consequences, adding more fuel to the already blazing inferno, a situation that is economically stifling for these less-developed countries and offering no respite in sight. Thus the more dependent these fragile economies are on the donor organizations, the more stringent the terms of the agreements become, with these countries continually pushed further and further away from the "core" of global economy. This inescapable phenomenon is what Cheryl (1974) termed the "debt trap."

The Liberal Economic Theory

The Liberal Economic Theory appears to offer a plausible argument on the debt crisis in developing countries, especially within the African subregion. Proponents of this theory argue that the implementation of economic liberalization and easing of trade and exchange restrictions is the way forward, in that this policy is able to facilitate the flow of foreign investments or capital to these developing countries. Here, the rationale is that homogenizing the political economy of every member state of the international community will provide a favorable environment, increasing the chances of creating a market society on a global scale (Biersteker, 1993).

One other major objective of economic liberalization will be to narrow the resource gap in these fragile economies by improving the existing trade balance between these countries and the donor industrial world, coupled with the encouragement of a net capital flow to these ailing economies. The fact that international organizations, such as the Group of Seven, the IMF, and World Bank, are attracting more recognition is indicative of the influence of liberal economic internationalism in the post–Cold War era (Biersteker, 1993). However, current fiscal events in these developing countries are a manifestation of attempts at restoring a more viable socioeconomic climate in the developing world by recommending greater foreign borrowing; but with it comes the unintended consequence in terms of the national debt of these countries in the developing world, which continues to expand with a concomitant increase in the resource gap. In fact, it is routine to see these fiscally powerful external institutions, which are proponents for the idea of free-trade liberalism, impose free-market limits on these developing societies. By so doing, these primary lender organizations, which have succeeded in entrenching formal and institutional market relationships between states, ultimately have peripheral states signing into agreements that are binding, forcing them to lower their protective barriers such as General Agreement on Tariffs and Trade (GATT) and North American Free Trade Agreement (NAFTA). This kind of fiscal maneuver prevents developing nations from mounting trade profiles that are not consistent with the model created and sponsored by the professed "comparative advantage" structures these institutions establish (Burchill et al., 1996). A case in point, the IMF and the World Bank formulate the provision of finance to developing societies predicated on the unilateral acceptance of free market rules for their economies, giving birth to the so-called structural adjustment program (SAP) that will be discussed in greater depth in the subsequent sections (Burchill et al., 1996).

The preconditions of the IMF, which have their theoretical roots in monetarist doctrines, do not demonstrate the slightest sensitivity to or consideration for to the unique, underdeveloped nature of these economies; and they might tell you that they are in business to make money if the obvious question of how they feel about dealing with these countries is raised. Rather, these prescriptions put in place by these institutions have had the effect of threatening the very survival of these already battered economies (Onimode, 1989). A case in point is one such prerequisite, where these donor institutions required the devaluation of local currencies in their economies as a precondition to capital flow. This represents a classic instance of external fiscal control and provides a vivid picture, at least in part, of the nature of the bond that these countries had no option but to establish. The application of this condition to countries such as Zambia in 1985 and Ghana and Nigeria in 1986 was meant to reap benefits for the long haul should these organizations decide to invest in these economies at later periods. This move put these already disturbed countries in a much weaker posture as they struggled to stay afloat. This maneuver raises the fundamental question about the merits of these institution-sponsored recommendations (Onimode, 1989).

In addition, there is a large element of uncertainty in the minds of the donor bodies regarding the capability and stamina of these countries to stem the tide of opposition to overall adjustment policies, which are crucial prerequisites for these countries to meet their loan repayment obligations. The Zambian and Nigerian experiences fit this profile. This simply means these institutions will contemplate how long these countries are able sustain these programs, considering how intense the terrain has been through the years and the magnitude of the strain they suffered following ratification of these fiscal agreements. This very likely explains why the donor institutions take a lackluster approach when dealing with these countries in Africa, especially those within the sub-Saharan region. The impression is that the maneuvers made by these financial institutions create a complex framework with which corrupt leaders in these developing economies find adequate cover to siphon off and deposit the already paltry financial resources of these nations into tax havens. The financial implications arising from this kind of behavior are obvious, with this being unacceptable and no doubt worsening the debt crisis and setting the stage for monumental insolvency and poverty (Ikejiaku, 2008, 2009). It is alleged that leaders such as former presidents Mobutu of the then Zaire (now the Democratic Republic of Congo) and Abacha and Babangida of Nigeria each may have embezzled sums of money of up to US$5 billion or more, and Arap Moi of Kenya, US$1 billion (Azami, 2005).

Therefore, it comes as no surprise that these struggling economies are constantly decapitalized and remain largely dependent on decisions made in New York, London, Paris, and other administrative or commercial centers in the industrialized world (Holsti, 1995). The fiscal lapses in these economies are an unequivocal verdict of a combination of these factors, which a section of the fiscal community believe created these ailing African economies and, hence, the insatiable need for financial support from the donor institutions through lending and other financial mechanisms on the part of these countries. Yet, manipulations by these financial institutions and other lending organizations, which were made feasible by the introduction of liberalism in Africa, had a negative impact on the purse or treasury of African countries, especially those within the sub-Saharan region, digging deeper into a debt crisis of huge proportions. The Nigerian experience is a classic case, where the Structural Adjustment Programs failed the majority of Nigerians, as it induced mass unemployment (AFRODAD, 2007) within the working class. Kenya has lamented its engagement with the IMF and the World Bank, which caused the country to change policies at the insistence of these institutions and which, by the way, was a unilateral push on the part of these institutions (Wayande, 1997).

In the early 1980s, countries such as Uganda were rocked by weeks of demonstrations, as industrial workers, other blue-collar workers, and students took to the streets to denounce former president Milton Obote's IMF-imposed economic program. The Benin situation was no different as former president Matthew Kerokou was overthrown following a wave of anti–Structural Adjustment Program riots (Dare, 2001). Using Botswana as an example of one of the few countries that rejected adjustment programs inspired by the IMF and World Bank, it can be argued that a country can perform very well in terms of economic growth (Hyden, 2000). Most scholars, such as Sachs (2005, p. 189), offer their own critique of the IMF and World Bank for imposing "draconian" budgets to support Structural Adjustment Programs in some developing countries, especially those countries south of the Sahara. Sachs questions the scientific merit and the benefits of this program and believes that even if there were any socioeconomic gains at all, they were minimal and not commensurate with the sacrifices these countries had to make.

Structural Adjustment Program

The term *Structural Adjustment Program* is used to describe the IMF and World Bank–inspired policy changes in the developing world. The Structural Adjustment Program was adopted by several sub-Saharan African countries with the aim of liberalizing their economies, particularly with regard to the external sector. The main purpose of trade liberalization was to promote economic growth by capturing the static and dynamic gains from trade through a more efficient allocation of resources, greater competition, and increase the flow of technology and investment, which ultimately accelerated the rate of capital accumulation and technical progress.

This "philosophy" of fiscal policy change, driven by the IMF and World Bank, contained terms by which any one of these countries that were willing to enroll had no option but to strictly abide. It was only when these conditions were met that these economies were able to implement a new loan package from the IMF and/or World Bank or qualify for lower interest rates on existing loans. The Structural Adjustment Programs were supposed to enable these ailing economies of the developing world become more market oriented, which then compels them to concentrate more on trade and production in order to boost their economies (Greenberg, 1997). Structural Adjustment Programs generally implement "free market" programs, both internal (notably privatization and deregulation) as well as external, of which the main one is the reduction of trade barriers (Babatunde, 2009).

Consequently, trade policies in most sub-Saharan African countries went through major changes within the framework of Structural Adjustment Programs during this period. As part of the program, foreign trade was liberalized through the reduction of tariffs and nontariff barriers as well as reduction of import duties applied to imports. Other provisions of the program included the abolition of import permits and lowering of duty rates, which form a part of tariff liberalization in many of these countries. Currencies of these countries were devalued on the premise that this fiscal maneuver would encourage exporters, boost exports and growth, as well as foster the integration of this African subregion into the global economy. A sizeable number of sub-Saharan African countries virtually eliminated parallel market premiums, with buying and selling of foreign exchange becoming market based and abolishing previous restrictions on currency transactions. The ultimate goal of this adjustment policy was to foster greater transparency, which would in turn boost economic growth and encourage the competitive integration of the economies of the subregion into the global economy (Babatunde, 2009).

Economists and other experts are divided on the impact of this policy change on these economies. Structural Adjustment Programs are considered by some scholars as packages of neoliberal free market–based economic policies that are fashioned and recommended to the developing world, such as the sub-Saharan region, to address the structural problems confronting these unhealthy economies. These programs are considered rapacious, with most social groups falling victim either directly and/or indirectly to measures, such as the withdrawal of subsidies on social services, retrenchment within the labor force, and the across-the-board increases in the prices of basic goods and services.

The Structural Adjustment Programs, together with the associated privatization that was embraced by a number of African countries such as Ghana, Zambia, Zimbabwe, and Tanzania, failed to rescue these countries from the grip of poverty and disease. Existing data demonstrate that the immediate outcome of this adjustment program had fallen into the negative, adversely impacting many social groups in these countries (Osei-Hwedie, 1992; Osei-Hwedie et al., 1992).

However, proponents of the Structural Adjustment Programs present these programs as the most viable strategy that had the capability to provide the much-needed momentum for a sustainable socioeconomic development in this subregion. Some pundits contended these programs generally involved the rolling back of the interventionist role of the administrations of these countries. The goal here was to reduce government's role by creating an enabling environment for investments by local and foreign capital (World Bank, 1981, 1989).

A few Structural Adjustment Program measures were thought by some scholars to be favorable to the development of spatially integrated economies in the sub-Saharan African region, including the provision of external loans to rehabilitate basic physical (facilities) and organizational (services) structures needed for the operation of simple systems, such as an enterprise, or more complex ones, such as a society or an economy for improved function. Ultimately, these measures, when put in place, were expected to revive and enhance industrial production and transportation processes. Sawyerr (1990, pp. 20–23) reported that the pattern of public expenditure is directed at the export sector, and the goal here is to generate foreign exchange through an incentive system that enables the related course of action.

These measures are sponsored by international financial institutions such as the IMF and the World Bank, World Bank internalists like Steel (1988) and Younger (1989), and academics such as Green (1987, 1991). These proponents identified a specific type of market failure caused by a deliberate government regulation that prevented economic agents from freely establishing a clearing price, which is in this case a market-distortion situation that constitutes a fundamental structural problem in the African subregion. These advocates contend that there is a loose association between the region's structural problems, their history of colonialism, and the form of integration into the world economy. Critics have contended that the economic maneuvers that these developing countries adopted, based on the recommendations of these institutions, had minimal intellectual basis and were practically counterproductive. Critics such as Sender (1999) have been critical of these institutions and question the merits of the outcome following the implementation of these policies. Sender further contends that the current level of public investment as a share of GDP in sub-Saharan Africa is paltry relative to the other regions around the world.

Other critics of Structural Adjustment Programs—academics such as Sawyerr (1990), Bromley (1995), and Owusu (1998a, 1998b) and world development organizations such as the United Nations Economic Commission for Africa—focused on the nature of the process by which economic growth and social development could be achieved. From their essentially structuralist viewpoint, these critics emphasized issues that included the need to restore equilibrium in terms of trade between the dependent countries and their industrial counterparts, as well as indigenous or domestic rather than external control of national socioeconomic destiny. In addition, critics' perspectives on the structural problems included linkages, where economic activities in different industries were linked to each other horizontally in the form of aggregate income and/or vertically in terms of input/output relationships within the African subregion, the lack of which spawned vicious cycles of underdevelopment. This vacuum, these critics argued, is the creation of two factors, the region's history of colonialism and the manner in which this subregion was integrated into the framework of the world economy. This was in contradiction to the primary objective of integration, which is to assist African economies in identifying and minimizing trade facilitation and related bottlenecks by combining detailed diagnostic studies with follow-up implementation efforts to alleviate the tremendous constraints facing many of these ailing economies. On the basis of the above, these critics held the perception that Structural Adjustment Programs were a subtle and convenient way for international capital and economically anxious governments to modulate the battered economies to meet their own political and economic interests (Ninsin, 1990; Owusu, 1995, 1998b).

It is apparent at this juncture that there was an unambiguous dissonance in the perspectives of proponents and critics on the expected outcomes associated with Structural Adjustment Programs and structural transformation within the subregion. The expectations of adjustment, proponents of this program believed, were rooted primarily in the concept of spatial/market equilibrium. This concept derived from the nature of the production pattern of both formal and informal sectors in this subregion as the result of postcolonial government intervention, which was considered unnecessary, excessive, and negligent (Engberg-Pedersen et al., 1996, p. 4). The proponents of this concept noted that the neglect of physical infrastructure and even the erratic nature of the informal sector relative to the formal represented constraints on development and were considered an outcome of state crisis and regulation.

On the basis of the position of the Structural Adjustment Programs proponents, addressing these primarily domestically created and bred structural problems required domestic housecleaning and the exploitation of domestic natural resources, for which these countries had comparative advantage, as the first step towards socioeconomic recovery (World Bank, 1981; Green, 1987, 1991). By so doing, the respective countries found a relative locus within the international division of labor (Hughes, 1980; Hawkins, 1986), rendering economies or countries more successful in achieving an overall economic growth however modest, given that these economies do not function in a vacuum but instead are integrated into the world economy. (Fischer, 1990; Krueger, 1992).

Use of international capital was necessary to resolve the issue of domestic lack of capital. In relation to the above positions, the proponents' expectations for the application of adjustment policies included an inevitable disruption of the preadjustment spatial structure, supplanted by an adjustment-based competitive market process, which ultimately balanced the production system. This pathway was expected to produce a new spatial pattern of economic activity with its associated linkage patterns that represented an activity pattern necessary for near-optimum economic efficiency (Simpson, 1994, p. 145).

The other benefits that proponents emphasized included the transformation of informal activities into formal operations via capital formation in the informal sector, facilitated by the enabling economic environment created by the government under the Structural Adjustment Program (de Soto, 1989; World Bank, 1989, pp. 135–136). Others included the infusion of foreign loans or structural adjustment loans/sectoral adjustment loans into the dependent economy, providing industry access to the necessary capital so as to achieve a more than baseline production to rendering them solvent (Ewusi, 1987, p. 13).

Finally, the problems associated with the basic physical and organizational structures within each one of these economies can be addressed through adjustment-based rehabilitation projects, such as road construction, improved distribution of electric power, and the development of reliable telecommunication systems (World Bank, 1984, p. 50). Critics, on the other hand, questioned the merits of these propositions, which proponents of adjustment believed, if implemented, would serve as a solid platform for the establishment of entities that market domestic natural resources, a move that would contribute to the overall development of the national economy. Far too little attention had been given to the accumulation of evidence suggesting a causal relationship between the macroeconomic stabilization programs of the IMF and the decline in investment ratios (Kraev, 2004).

The establishment of this association between the external institution and these fragile economies meant that African countries' exports remained concentrated in a few primary commodities, whose prices are notoriously volatile. Taylor (1988) classifies these countries that underwent structural adjustment in the "externally strangled small primary product or labor exporters" category, to which all African countries belong. As Deaton (1999) pointed out, the variance of price could equal several times the variance of supply as a result of price-inelastic demand functions for primary commodities. In other words, the prices of commodities varied much more and at a higher rate (on the plus side) while marginal changes were recorded for supply.

Also, critics of the program were of the view that orthodox Structural Adjustment Programs tend to focus only on the economistic standpoint and failed to recognize that the cause(s) of economic decline are broad. However, critics concede that these adjustment-based programs may be valid in well-structured economies and that the theory of comparative advantage, which serves as the basis for Structural Adjustment Programs, was designed for countries with comparable levels of industrialization (Amin, 1990; Barker et al., 1986). Hence, countries in the developing world do not represent candidates suitable enough for this form of intervention for economic recovery based on the fragile and disjointed structures associated with adjustment (UN/ECA, 1986, p. 1; Bromley, 1995).

As a consequence, policies based on comparative advantage were inherently flawed for underdeveloped countries in the sub-Saharan African region, especially for those who faced unfavorable terms of trade where imports from the developed world were uncontrolled. Opponents of this program were troubled as they wondered what would become of the existing formal-informal sector when the Structural Adjustment Programs were implemented. Ninsin (1991) reports that it is the formal sector in these countries that gave rise to an informal sector, which provided goods and services necessary for the economies of these countries without formal controls and compensation. This status quo represented the failure of capitalism to transform the sub-Saharan African economies. The informal sector is therefore seen as a dependable entity of the formal sector, just as developed nations have devised mechanisms to exploit the developing ones. In the case of formal-informal sector relations, the mechanisms ensured that formal sector operators or firms were able to accumulate at the expense of the informal sector operators because of the lower production and distribution cost that their links with the latter enables them to achieve (Ninsin, 1991, p. 5).

Critics of the adjustment programs believe that countries that embraced these programs were also compelled to accommodate foreign capital under the terms of the liberalization measures that these programs put in place. Hamilton saw these adjustments as a neocolonial mechanism intended to open up the adjustment economies and their markets to Western business interests (Hamilton, 1989). As part of the package, an export incentive system was put in place aimed at boosting the export of unprocessed materials or semifinished products to international markets only for the formal sector firms, which tend to foreclose potential linkages (Owusu, 1995). For example, systematic promotion of the export of processed wood products, such as lumber and furniture parts, and the dynamics of the free-market system within the Ghanaian economy could diminish the domestic traditional forward linkage systems on the basis that these exports are in several respects primary products, which simply means the production and market conditions of these exports are similar to that of primary products (Roemer, 1981, p. 432). Ultimately, these miniature firms were denied full benefits as they became components of a vertically organized and integrated conglomerate. (Sayer, 1986, pp. 47–48). Other units of the informal sector, such as the cocoa industry, undoubtedly fell victim to this kind of maneuver by these international firms. Also, the flexible exchange rate system hurt the linkage patterns in wood processing and other industries via easy access to cheaper inputs (Sawyerr, 1990, p. 33).

Additionally, the formal sector firms were inclined to exploit the informal sector in order to stay in business with capital that would enable the former enough control over its own episodic crisis (Weiss, 1987; Meagher, 1995). This mechanism was possible because, under the free-market conditions, contractual relations as established gained currency under the term of agreement and required informal-sector operators to supply the formal-sector firms with raw materials, or at best, semifinished goods (Ninsin, 1991, p. 4; Moser, 1978). Furthermore, the rehabilitation of physical infrastructure under the terms of the Structural

Adjustment Programs provided the Western industrialized countries a comparative advantage over these dependent countries of the African subregion. These investments inevitably required these countries to import heavy equipment and engage consultants and contractors from the industrialized countries who were the overt proponents of these adjustment programs. This kind of maneuver ultimately swelled the debt burden of the adjusting economies and, in most cases, the most viable pathway to meet this financial obligation was to use the revenue derived from their exports, leading to a huge trade gap. This was to be anticipated because the exports from these adjustment countries attracted much less monetary value compared to their imports.

The development of this infrastructure tended to favor projects that were export related, such as the rehabilitation of harbors, railways, and road networks, which inevitably required huge sums of money, thus becoming a powerful vacuum that sucked up a disproportionate fraction of this kind of public investment. In fact, these projects undoubtedly are written into the terms of the adjustment program, and there was no turning back following bilateral ratification. With this commitment firmly in place, these adjusting countries had no option but to abide by the terms of the agreement, and, by so doing, a trade deficit was born (Sawyerr, 1990, p. 33). The next segment will provide us with a glimpse of the policy profiles these donor institutions crafted in response to the debt crisis and the abject socioeconomic climate within the developing world, as well as the desired changes these policies were design to engender.

International Monetary Fund Adjustment Program

The primary goal of the Structural Adjustment Program, formulated by the IMF institutions, was to provide support to these ailing economies in the developing world. However, their modes of operation or policies in general portray these conglomerates as prowling entities looking for a soft target. The IMF loan scheme focused on providing a temporal fix to financial problems in economically constrained countries by lending to those countries that had balance of payment problems or were so insolvent that they were unable to fulfill their financial obligations in terms of their international debts. Currently, there are several versions of the IMF loan package in terms of the duration that these loans have to be paid back. There are the short-term loans that are repaid between two and one-half and four years following the ratification of the agreement; there are long-term options available for up to seven years (UN MDG Report, 2007) but are less frequently offered compared to the short-term loans. The other tier involves loans granted to countries in the event of natural disasters such as flooding or earthquake, or conflict. Over the decades, the central policy of the IMF was centered on stabilization. This policy prescription was fashioned in an attempt to reduce trade deficits mainly in terms of volume of imports by minimizing privatization and public, private, and partnerships' demand for final goods and services in these economies at any given time and price level. This fund utilized the mechanisms available to hold inflation in check, but this was often less amenable to policy control. Austerity from the fiscal and monetary standpoints dominated IMF programs, which when implemented exerted a lowering effect on the growth of the GDP of a given economy. On the flipside, this fiscal and monetary action may have reduced the rate of inflation and guaranteed a reduction in imports. As part of the agreement, the IMF recommended the following: a decrease in public spending coupled with high interest rates on loans the government could grant, a fiscal instrument that was expected to boost savings, and discipline in providing credit facilities, especially for the public sector. Indicators such as the permissible growth of the money supply and the proportion of the fiscal deficit to GDP served as the gauge for measuring the performance of the adjustment programs these countries adopted and implemented. In addition, this institution recommended an exchange rate adjustment, which came at a cost. The profiles of these struggling economies, configured by the fund, allowed the nominal exchange rate enough momentum to drive the ailing system through several channels, such as trade deficits, which could be reduced by devaluing the local currency. The trade-off was that this policy ultimately drove up profits accrued from exports and made imports more expensive. The consequence of this measure took the form of a slow export response, which then meant that purchasing power was limited in the face of stratospheric prices of internal goods and services, creating a contractionary situation that led to aggregate demand. This measure had serious political implications within the country, setting the stage for an upheaval, an outcome that had the potential to disrupt the program.

It must be emphasized that these ailing economies risked perturbations within the capital market in cases where external trade and capital activities assumed the pendulum motion as they had the flexibility to swing back and forth. This climate then transformed the exchange rate into an asset price, which foreign investors monitored very closely. This level of scrutiny was absolutely crucial because quick and prudent determinations had to be made as to the direction of the flow of funds within the economy. In the case of real exchange appreciation, the slightest weakening of the trade account will automatically require a deployment of steps necessary to secure capital inflow by raising real internal interest rates. This results in the ill effects of investment demand, which is determined by how much investment businesses decide to undertake, as well as capital buildup. This maneuver, in terms of currency devaluation, reduced the foreign currency value of the existing national assets that these investors already held or decided to pull out of these countries. In the long term, they stood to make huge gains in future acquisitions that came at a much lower cost.

The World Bank Adjustment Program

The primary objective of the World Bank is to increase the IMF by instilling adjustments in these struggling economies through market friendliness. The World Bank, unlike the IMF, offers loans to fund particular development projects, such as the physical and/or organizational infrastructure within the economy. In effect, World Bank Structural Adjustment Programs tend to focus on providing loans and grants to countries on a project-by-project basis. The World Bank is divided into two lending and development institutions: the International Bank for Reconstruction and Development and the International Development Association. The former focuses on "middle income and credit-worthy poor countries" while the latter focuses on the "lowest income and least credit worthy countries" (World Bank, 2008).

The agenda set by the World Bank was to improve the efficiency of allocation within a given economy by improving the capability of the economy to provide the citizens with the amounts and types of goods and services that they most preferred. In standard economic theory this situation will prevail only when resources are allocated in such a way that any change in the amounts or types of outputs currently being produced would reduce the quality of life of the citizens. This is on the basis that eliminating price "distortions," such as slashing artificially high real wages, will yield dividends in that companies that produce goods or provide services will be in a better position to hire more workers. It was anticipated that such a step could boost industrial production. On the flipside, this proposition appeared to have minimal empirical footing in the sense that a negative correlation between wages and industrial output is seldom observed in a real-world situation. In fact, the more likely scenario is a direct correlation between the two variables, and the trend is downward for both of them when such a measure is implemented. Akin to devaluation, the political implications could derail the program to the core if wage cuts were implemented in order to reduce effective demand that is expected to build greater income concentration.

Bank-sponsored adjustment packages that were recommended in an attempt to improve resource allocation assumed several forms, including the situation where the World Bank advocated for liberalization of foreign trade beginning with replacement of import quotas by tariffs, which were then followed by a reduction in tariffs and export subsidies. By driving relative internal prices closer to world levels, these maneuvers were expected to support exports through cost reductions and to increase outputs for the same resources, or have the same or better results achieved for fewer resources, leading to efficiency gains, but there are just a few such cases on record (Helleiner, 1995).

Another version of the World Bank package came in the form of a support system where this institution, simultaneously or shortly after, put in place a reduction in barriers to external capital flows, such as controls on foreign exchange transactions and profit remittances, paving the way for external suppliers of funds for investment in the target economy. The World Bank appears to have directed attention away from the fact that, until very recently, foreign money could be withdrawn at the same rate at which it was infused.

One other recommendation the World Bank made to these countries was deregulation or "derepression" of the home financial market. The goal here was to even out the rate of return or return on investment (which in this case is the amount of money gained or lost relative to what was invested) to different financial assets or capital. The aim of this move was to rescue interest rates that have been held down or "repressed" as a subsidy to borrowers in anticipation of stimulating savings. Unfortunately, this measure was unable to produce any desired empirical outcome and was therefore jettisoned.

Other options on the table included the deregulation of labor markets and business decision making and the rationalization of taxes. These ailing economies of the sub-Saharan region appeared to be good candidates for a proposition where hikes were introduced to the system so as to provide a financial base that is crucial to civil-service reforms. Unfortunately, these countries at that time practiced the "spoils system," where the party in power offered especially elite job positions to contributors and other sympathizers, a culture that posed a threat to this program. Also, the intended pathway for the implementation of this kind of measure, in the case of Ghana and Uganda, appeared to have been motivated by their central governments instead of the private sectors, leading to an overreach of the central government in these economies.

It was against this background that the World Bank subsequently decided to direct its focus on privatization of public enterprises, which was rooted in the premise that privately owned enterprises are intrinsically more efficient than parastatal firms. This proposition appeared to have ignited some level of uneasiness upon close examination by scholars such as Chang and Singh (1993). A cross-section of pundits was of the opinion that selling off state-owned firms often amounts to a fiscal stop-gap measure to close budget deficits that were created by rapid tax reductions. Finally, by reducing government overreach and corruption, as well as infusing more transparency within the economy, liberalization and privatization are expected to channel resources to more viable and productive projects. However, reports by Boratav, Turel, and Yeldan (1996) showed that the very people in power and their cohort, such as the bourgeoisie in most of these Third World countries, were the creations of the country.

In effect, while both the IMF and World Bank provided loans to financially challenged developing countries, the modus operandi of these institutions, in an attempt to salvage these weak economies, assumes different forms.

Chapter Five
The Ghanaian Situation

Preadjustment Economy

In the years immediately preceding adjustment, Ghana's total IMF growth rate was –14.9 percent on the scale, with an annual average of –5.2 percent (Huq, 1989, p. 46). According to World Bank estimates, by April 1983 the country's outstanding external debt, when the adjustment program was initiated, totaled as much as US$1.12 billion (disbursed) and US$1.50 billion (undisbursed), with a total interest payment of US$38.7 million (World Bank, 1985, p. 33). By the beginning of 1983, the county's ravaged economy was aptly described in *The Economist* (1989, p. 40) as an abject situation even by Africa's standards. According to Engberg-Pederson et al. (1996, p. 11), this extreme macroeconomic tsunami in the making was primarily the result of reckless financial stewardship spanning a period of almost two decades. Exchange-rate overvaluation and high taxes imposed on exports inflicted a direct hit on exports such as cocoa, timber, and gold from the mid-1970s, leading to a precipitous downtrend with very little hope of stopping the free fall. Additionally, external factors coupled with an outrageously large public spending deficit increased the rate of inflation to a whopping 80 percent or more per annum. With the dismal performance of the country's economy and an economic volcano waiting to erupt, the administration of the Provisional National Defense Council, like many others in heavily indebted developing countries, became less stringent in engaging Western economies and financial institutions and began to do business with foreign lenders on an exclusively bilateral basis. Like other ailing economies, Ghana suffered a financial syndrome with the allure of foreign loans, uneasiness from its fiscal crises, and a balance of payments deficit facing the possibility of being declared insolvent by the IMF and the World Bank as the manifestations (Ould-Mey, 1996, pp. 15–16). This set the stage, and rightfully so, for the easy promotion of IMF and World Bank–inspired policies called the Structural Adjustment Programs, an attractive treatment protocol from these lender institutions. Structural Adjustment Programs were implemented around the strategy of providing loans to the country and other ailing economies, a financial tango that paved the way for the World Bank and the IMF to launch an economic takeover and subsequently dictate socioeconomic policies to these countries.

Economic Reforms

Structural Adjustment Programs—or structural adjustment policies, as some scholars may choose to describe them—began to appear in the early 1980s. Ghana adopted the World Bank/IMF–inspired Structural Adjustment Programs and other measures, which will be discussed in later sections, in response to the deteriorating socioeconomic situation in the country, which began to manifest in the 1970s. These reform programs involved economic liberalization and privatization as well as a general restructuring of government's role in the economy. In the case of Ghana, a section of the academic community was of the opinion that the Structural Adjustment Program, which was adopted by the then Provisional National Defense Council administration, was nothing but a metonym (Ninsin, 1990). The primary goal, as scholars believed at that time, was to prevent a domestic political and economic crisis that was waiting to happen, at least in the short term. These reforms consisted of a framework of economic liberalization and privatization and a general restructuring of the country's economy. Although there was some benefit to the implementation of this model that was recommended by these institutions, as some economic growth on the macroeconomic level was recorded, this benefit still came with a high social cost.

For critics, Structural Adjustment Programs would simply not fashion a spatially integrated economy with its associated dynamic sectoral linkage structure in Ghana, especially with the elimination of government intervention, which they consider indispensable for the desired economic transformation (Mytelka, 1989; Bromley, 1995). There were other critics who saw the change in policy as a mere political calculation aimed at precluding the collapse of the administration. They were of the view that the potential political disaster would be due in part to the government's failure to embrace what they termed "international capital" and called for the transfer of funds from private individuals, companies, and/or governments that were idle to other entities within the country facing a shortage of funds in anticipation of promoting economic efficiency. Alongside this prescription, these scholars suggested that the government provide a climate where labor and resources would be open to exploitation in situ, while at the same time supplying raw materials and other input needed by the Western industrialized economies as well as providing markets for their products (Sawyerr, 1990, p. 28).

Although the implementation of the measures prescribed by the IMF and World Bank appeared to have provided some momentum for economic growth, at least at the macroeconomic level, this marginal advancement came at a high social cost. This assertion by some scholars is believed to be structured on the fact that most vulnerable groups were adversely affected both directly and indirectly as a result of measures such as the withdrawal of subsidies on social services, retrenchment of labor, and the general increases in prices of goods or services. (Adepoju, 1993; Sowa, 1993; Donkor, 1997; Konadu-Agyemang, 2000). Another wave of criticism of the Structural Adjustment Programs in Ghana suggested that not only were the benefits of adjustment modest for several years following implementation, but the socioeconomic gains were limited to the traditional resource-rich regions in the southern belt of the country, which had a high concentration of cocoa and coffee plantations, mining, and logging activities. This asymmetrical distribution of the modest gains of adjustment was discriminatory and eventually widened the socioeconomic gap between the northern and southern parts of the country (Songsore and Denkabe, 1995). Proponents like the then first lady, Nana Konadu Agyemang-Rawlings, and Adanu held a different viewpoint and were of the opinion that the data available at that time did not support this assertion by the critics. These proponents believed that the promotion of nontraditional export commodities under Structural Adjustment Programs offered the northern communities a fair share of participation in export trade—a process, they asserted, that would have a positive impact on the previously economically disadvantaged northern regions in the long run, if adequate stewardship was put in place along with the necessary physical and organizational structures (Konadu-Agyemang and Adanu, 2003).

Ofori (2002) reports that the infrastructural improvements following the implementation of the Structural Adjustment Programs at the national and regional levels are a clear manifestation of the commitment to increase rural accessibility, improve rural-urban linkages, and facilitate the transport of regional and local agricultural produce. In recent years, the Structural Adjustment Programs–induced improvement in the transportation system, with the road sector enjoying most of the donor-funded programs, had contributed significantly to the growth of both large and small towns. Liberalization and privatization (deregulation of public transport) had seen the partial demolition of the barriers of physical distance within the past few decades following the Structural Adjustment Programs due to an increase in the private commercial transport component officially designated as the Ghana Private Road Transport Union. The resumption of the flow of financial aid coupled with the removal of many foreign exchange barriers facilitated the importation of motor vehicles and accessories to various parts of Ghana and other African countries (Bryceson, 2001). So while analysts such as Briggs and Yeboah (1969) have attributed the expansion of Ghana's major urban centers, such as the Accra metropolitan area, to adjustment policies, it can also be argued that economic liberalization and privatization have improved linkages between settlements, allowing rural dwellers access to higher-order centers (large and medium-sized towns) and vice versa (Briggs and Yeboah, 2001). This improvement in linkages, coupled with other infrastructural components, introduced some forms of economic activities such as the provision of services and nonagricultural goods, which were nonexistent preadjustments in smaller towns.

The Structural Adjustment Programs enjoyed additional support from other experts whose contention in favor of the programs is rooted in the inflation rate, removal of subsidies (which for a long time largely benefited the urban population), and the shrinking of the formal sector (which was largely concentrated in the larger urban centers). This resulted in urban unemployment and an accompanying high cost of living in these centers, leading to the loss of some of the glamour the urban communities once enjoyed, thereby rendering these cities and towns less attractive to rural dwellers whose economic activities are dominated by subsistence agriculture (Acheampong, 1996; Aeroe, 1992; Burrows, 1992; Owusu, 2002, 2005a).

In a related argument, Gilbert reported that Structural Adjustment Programs led to reductions in rural–urban migration rates and a consequent reduction in the growth of major cities, while at the same time permitting the growth of both secondary cities and other locations in the national urban system (Briggs and Yeboah, 2001). Some authors have even indicated that not only has this policy change limited the rural-urban switch but has actually changed the direction of the tide (Canagarajah and Mazumdar, 1997; Sowa, 1993; GSS, 1995). Gilbert provides three possible explanations that include the diseconomies of scale, the forces that cause larger firms to produce goods and services at increased per-unit costs. These are normally associated with major cities coupled with the overall improvements in transportation, and other levels of the infrastructure scale may have resulted in the deconcentration of manufacturing and other economic activities. Another explanation Gilbert offers entails the shifting terms of trade from industrial production to raw agricultural material, a change that has favored rural communities, allowing its inhabitants more economically attractive activities. This shift, Gilbert proposes, has favored Structural Adjustment Programs–inspired export-oriented trade agriculture over industry, a situation that has compelled investors to change course and relocate outside the core of the Third World metropolis (Gilbert, 1993).

While the explanations put forward by Gilbert may hold true for other Third World countries, especially in Latin America, some scholars believe these elucidations do not apply to the Ghanaian situation (Yeboah, 2000). Available evidence suggests that Structural Adjustment Programs in Ghana have in fact not facilitated deconcentration of industries and employment or have had a significant shift in the terms of trade in favor of agriculture. Instead, the core metropolitan areas, especially those of Accra and Tema in the Greater Accra Region of the country, have continued to dominate in terms of investments within the country. One of the visible impacts of Structural Adjustment Programs in Ghana is the dramatic rise in industrial activities, particularly of foreign companies, within the Accra metropolis (Grant and Yankson, 2003). In all, the Accra-Tema metropolis accounts for approximately 70 percent of the country's manufacturing output, which is comparable to Andræ's pre–Structural Adjustment Programs estimate of manufacturing units in Ghana (Andræ, 1981).

Data from the 2000 Population and Housing Census Reports indicate that the country's four major urban communities, Accra, Tema, Kumasi, and Sekondi-Takoradi, all in the southern and coastal belts, account for approximately 44 percent of the total urban population. Accordingly, a Ghana Statistical Service report on the census noted that a balanced spatial distribution of the population is not likely to be achieved unless the opportunities for improvement in the lives of the people are distributed more evenly. Alternatively, the average income of the various urban systems in the country could be assessed through data generated by some studies on poverty. A well-controlled study by the Ghana Statistical Service,

"Poverty Trends in Ghana in the 1990s," demonstrates that even though there was a general downward trend in the incidence and level of poverty within the country in the 1990s (except for the urban north), the decline was precipitous in Accra (GSS, 2000; Konadu-Agyemang, 2000) compared to other urban centers. Notwithstanding the modest gains of the Structural Adjustment Programs with regard to the growth of small towns, it can be argued that this improvement in the infrastructural base of rural areas and lower urban centers in terms of electrification projects as well as road construction and rehabilitation under the Structural Adjustment Programs have rendered these remote parts of the country more accessible, with the rural dwellers enjoying facilities long considered an urban privilege. After all, these communities constitute the cradle of agricultural and logging activities that cater to both domestic and foreign markets.

Adjustment and Forest Resources in Ghana

It was against this background that the World Bank made recommendations to the then Provisional National Defense Council government at the initial stages of the adjustment program to direct more attention to the forestry sector. This recommendation was based on three reasons. First, the forestry sector and its constituent formal wood-processing industry constitute an important component of the Ghanaian economy. Second, this sector was considered one that had the potential to provide the highest immediate returns for economic growth and foreign exchange earnings. And finally, reviving this sector meant a restoration of one of the major rural economic activities, especially within the southern belt of the country. In the past, the forestry sector accounted for approximately 5–6 percent of Ghana's IMF and 11 percent of commodity export earnings. At that time, it represented the third most important sector for commodity exports, after cocoa and mineral resources.

With the economic meltdown in the early 1980s, this sector took a severe hit and sunk to its lowest level in 1982. The exports from this sector yielded a paltry US$15.3 million in external revenue that year, several times less than the revenue of US$136 million that was accrued almost a decade earlier (TEDB, s.d., p. 15). Although this sector had an immense potential for linkages, the preadjustment linkage patterns of this industry painted a detailed picture of how abject spatial integration had become. Notwithstanding the posture of this sector at that time, both the government and the World Bank were confident that a modest infusion of capital into this sector could result in a disproportionately greater output within a short time span, a fiscal move considered to have the potential to provide a win-win outcome for both the government and World Bank (Owusu, 1998b). Knowing that this sector was the goose that lays the golden eggs, the government infused a capital of US$157 million (World Bank Loan) into this sector at the beginning of the adjustment program, with the objective of stabilizing this sector and driving output into positive territory (Ofei-Nkansah, 1991).

Integrated into the world capitalist system as a British colony, Ghana served both as a source of raw forest materials and a market for finished manufactured added-value products. Within that asymmetrical relationship with the colonial masters at that time, the dynamic sectors of the colony's economy were calibrated to align with British economic interests (Sawyerr, 1990, p. 10). This structural legacy of the British colonial system, as Mabogunje (1981, p. 2) suggested, was what rendered the country devoid of crucial independence and fundamental self-interest. Ultimately, the country's economy, following political independence, developed the characteristics of foreign dependence and regional inequities, a situation compounded by weak inter- and intrasectoral linkages (Darkoh, 1971, 1973), which Szerezewski (1966, p. 66) described as "perhaps the very essence of under-development." This scenario became obvious in that the country had become dependent on imports for intermediate and capital goods (Darkoh, 1973, p. 9). Combé (1972, pp. 4–5), reported that approximately a third of the foreign exchange generated by export of lumber had to be used for the import of machinery and related accessories.

Adjustment and Agriculture in Ghana

The World Development Report underscored the fundamental role agriculture can play if the Millennium Development Goal of reducing the share of people suffering from extreme poverty and hunger by 50 percent by the year 2015 is to be achieved (World Development Report, 2008). The report goes further to accentuate the fact that in much of sub-Saharan Africa, agriculture is crucial to building a strong prospect for stimulating economic growth, reducing poverty, enhancing food security, and stimulating growth in other sectors of the economy (World Development Report, 2008). This is supported by existing data on countries that are agriculture based, demonstrating that the agricultural sector in most of these countries, especially those in the sub-Saharan region of Africa, generate on average 29 percent of the GDP and employ 65 percent of the labor force, most of whom are rural dwellers (World Development Report, 2008). Unfortunately, it has been reported that rural areas in this African subregion account for 75 percent of people who live on less than US$1 a day, with most of this group depending directly or indirectly on agricultural activities for their livelihoods (UNDP Human Development Report, 2007).

The message these numbers convey is unequivocal, and therefore the need for a marginal change in the short term, or a radical overhaul of this sector in the long term, cannot be overemphasized. The 2008 World Development Report indicates that accelerated growth in this sector depends heavily on the establishment of an effective support system to cater to the millions engaged in subsistence agriculture, many of whom live in the rural areas. Only when this policy is put in place and implemented will there be an increase in productivity in smallholder farming (World Development Report, 2008).

Ghana was one of the first countries in sub-Saharan Africa to initiate a program of economic stabilization and market reform under the Economic Recovery Program, which was under the supervision of the IMF and the World Bank. The goal of this drive was to harmonize the economic imbalances and distortions that contributed to the stagnation and decline of the economy through the 1970s to the early 1980s. Prior to the inception of this recovery program, Ghana, very much like most of the sub-Saharan African countries, had in place restrictive and distortionary agricultural policies dating back to the time the country attained political independence from the British colonial masters. Aryeetey et al. (2000) have reported that one area of the country's economy that has enjoyed much attention in the economic reform process is trade and agricultural liberalization, a testament to the pivotal role these play in economic growth within the country. It does not come as a surprise that the 2008 United Nations Economic and Social Council report suggested that the rural environment, which accounts for over 60 percent of the country's land mass, was pivotal to the national economic transformation. The framework of agriculture in Ghana has always been designed with the goal of increasing food production in order to ensure adequate food security and nutrition and to provide raw materials and other inputs for the other sectors of the economy whose activities require agricultural raw materials (Brooks et al., 2006). This sector of the economy underwent several rounds of modification, first introduced in 1983, during which time agricultural activities were ravaged by severe drought and wildfires in most parts of the country that continued up to the 1990s.

Before the introduction of these modifications, parastatals were firmly in place, underscoring the role of government at the beginning of the postindependence period. Policies that were formulated during that period reiterated the need for modernization of agriculture and expansion through major capital investments under the control of the Ghanaian government. This led to the establishment of what came to be known as "State Farms," which assumed a monumental scale that required large tracts of land across the country and intense labor to undertake a program of this magnitude. The early 1970s observed a modest change in course when the government shifted focus, deciding that engaging private entrepreneurs could be a viable option. Subsequently, state-owned enterprises, machinery, and equipment were sold to private entrepreneurs. The transition was gradual with experiments on import liberalization emphasizing small-scale agricultural development alongside large state farms within the framework of the government's economic programs. The report goes further, indicating that a transformation of the rural environment was dependent heavily on agro-based industrialization, which entailed agricultural processing, effective decentralization, private-sector development, and a scale-back of the government's role in this sector.

One other area that was vital to this transformation, as the report recommended, was the process of land policy reform to make land acquisition easier, thereby ensuring a more efficient land-ownership and title process. To increase the area of land under irrigation, a boost in mechanized agriculture, expansion of cash crop production (traditional crops such as cocoa and cashews), development of marketing channels for agricultural produce, and increased financial support for the private sector were part of the reform effort by the government (United Nations Economic and Social Council [ECOSOC], 2008). Even though commercial agriculture was central to the reform strategy, it was imperative to invest in smallholder agriculture, at least in the short term. The strategy was to emphasize labor-intensive as opposed to capital-intensive technologies by promoting simple, mechanized agricultural practices to reduce drudgery; rural over urban locations of processing plants for agricultural produce; and encouraging the cultivation of crops that can be produced by most smallholders (ECOSOC). The deployment of this effort was to make agriculture attractive to the rural folk, which in turn was expected to sequester the rural population and ultimately limit out-migration to the urban communities.

Some of the challenges this program encountered were associated with the creation of land banks and agri-business zones. In addition, the effort at recruiting extension staff meant for rural agricultural activities only yielded a marginal reduction in the attrition rate of these officers, with the extension officer–farmer improving from 1:1500 in 2002 to 1:1400 in 2005 (ECOSOC).

The fisheries subsector was not left out of the program. This subsector made the list of areas in the agricultural sector that were earmarked for rehabilitation with emphasis on aquaculture. These policies hinged mainly on the reduction of harvest losses, the increase of crop production, and the building of silos, which the United Nations Economic and Social Council estimated would show positive trends over the cost of implementation. In addition, the program was aimed at reducing post-harvest losses, which appeared to have improved from approximately 25 to 15 percent for cereals, and 40 to 35 percent for perishables as a result of the installation of more processing equipment. Estimates following a survey of 2,081 households engaged in agriculture showed that 53–86 percent of this group reported an improvement in the accessibility of storage and processing equipment, a testament to the numbers recorded for the perennial post-harvest loses. This sector saw an increase in the size of arable land under irrigation by 58 percent. The rehabilitation of the fisheries subsector showed that the quantity of fingerlings produced per annum increased from 150,000 in 2002 to a staggering 6,900,000 in 2005, while the area under fish farming saw a boost from 112 hectares in 2002 to 350 hectares in 2005.

Notwithstanding these numbers from the United Nations Economic and Social Council report and other reports, the effect of the adjustment and other reform programs on Ghana's agricultural sector has attracted conflicting opinions from economists in industry, policy, and academia. Some reports suggest that Ghana's agricultural sector, which is dominated by the rural community, and rightly so, was adversely impacted right from the inception of IMF and World

Bank–inspired adjustment programs, although they admitted the spirit of the program was legitimate.

The changes in policy that led to the removal of price distortions on crops—eliminating the guaranteed minimum price paid to farmers for food crops such as maize and rice, subsidies on agricultural inputs, and especially a formulated quick-release form of soil amendments—amounting to the reduction of parastatals and a scale-back of government's role in this sector were considered counterproductive by some scholars (Nyanteng and Seini, 2000). These authors went further to infer that these drastic modifications comprised the underlying factors responsible in part for nonperformance of this sector, which manifested in decreased productivity, especially for food crops (Nyanteng and Seini, 2000). In their view, these modifications created a vacuum in the process of procurement, supply, and distribution of agricultural inputs, coupled with the failure of the private sector to assume such responsibilities at the incipient stage. The limitation on logistics set off a chain reaction causing a dramatic spike in the real prices of critical agricultural inputs, such as fertilizers, insecticides, and fungicides.

Other experts are of the opinion that the way forward in revitalizing agriculture requires a sharp U-turn in policy, where public funding is applied to the construction and rehabilitation of new and existing roads and the establishment of schools, health centers, and agricultural extension services in these communities. The effectiveness of agricultural education and research should be expanded to ensure a strong partnership between farmers and economists as well as other related experts. Very likely, the most important requirement, as the authors indicate, is equity of the price of agricultural produce for farmers. Although the tenets of the Structural Adjustment Program comprised normalizing exchange rates, privatizing state-owned companies, and liberalizing internal markets, these were considered irrelevant as long as the farmers faced price inequities on the world market (Anderson and Martin, 2006).

Another school of thought entailed agrarian (major rural or semirural economic activities such as such as farming, fishing, or ranching) depression as very refractory and therefore unresponsive to the application of any kind of fix. On the basis of this, the sponsors of this proposal saw it as more beneficial to infuse resources into more "viable" sectors of the economy, such as the service and trade sector, that will be capable of absorbing the horde of out-migrants who have abandoned agriculture in search of more viable alternatives (Anderson and Martin, 2006).

It must be emphasized that policies affecting this sector can be politically and economically sensitive and sometimes beyond the control of some governments, with self-interest and lobbying groups who display the tendency to suggest sidelining trade negotiations altogether, as it has been in numerous subglobal preferential trading agreements such as GATT, a former specialized agency of the United Nations, prior to the Uruguay Round. By the way, in 1995, GATT was transformed into what is today the World Trade Organization. GATT, which was created following the conclusion of World War II, was implemented to further regulate world trade to facilitate economic recovery following the war. The main objective of GATT was to reduce the barriers of international trade through the reduction of tariffs, quotas, and subsidies, and to eliminate discriminatory treatment in international commerce. Such a wide exchange of concessions was intended to promote free trade, although there has been some criticism of the principle of equal trading opportunities on the grounds that establishment of free trade tends to favor the economically advantaged countries. GATT members recognized, in principle, that the most-favored-nation clause ensures equal commercial opportunities, especially concerning import duties, and that freedom of investment should be relaxed to accommodate the needs of developing countries. The 1964 United Nations Conference on Trade and Development sought to extend preferential treatment to the exports of the developing countries. Another challenge to the most-favored-nation clause was posed by regional trading groups such as the European Union, which lowered or eliminated tariffs among members while maintaining tariff walls between member nations and the rest of the world.

Today, the groups with the proclivity to relegate issues regarding equity in the international market for agricultural produce at such conferences include not just farmers in the highly protected countries and net-food-importing developing countries, but also those food exporting nations receiving preferential access to those markets, including holders of tariff rate quotas, members of regional trading agreements, and parties to nonreciprocal preference agreements, including all least developed countries. However, it was argued that pushing agriculture to the sidelines in the Doha Development Round (2001) would do a major disservice to many of the world's poorest people, especially those in farm households in developing countries. The implications are obvious because agricultural earnings are so crucial to almost all countries in the developing world that the highly protective farm policies the few wealthy countries seek to entrench have become targets by these developing countries in subsequent World Trade Organization negotiations, with greater access to markets in the industrial world for their farm produce a high priority for them. Currently, the European Union's provisions for former colonies in Africa, the Caribbean, and Pacific program, and, more recently, for Least Developed Countries under the Everything But Arms agreement, the United States' Africa Growth and Opportunity Act, and the Caribbean Basin Initiative are some of the schemes through which some developing countries gained greater access to developed-country markets for a selection of products under various preferential agreements. Not only have these schemes reduced demands for developed-country farm policy reform from preference-receiving countries but they also have exacerbated the concerns of other countries excluded from these programs, thus worsening the economic plight of these countries in terms of declining terms of trade, and, to some degree, aggravated rather than improved aggregate global welfare as well as the socioeconomic welfare of developing countries.

Although the Uruguay Round of 1994 agreed to a range of trade negotiations, including a dramatic reduction in tariffs and agricultural subsidies, an agreement to allow full access to textiles and clothing from developing countries, and an extension of intellectual property rights, many of the developing countries perceived it as unsatisfactory and that the talks failed to provide them with a good deal.

From a mercantilistic view, these developing countries believed that some of their industrial counterparts sought to advance a protectionist agenda by encouraging exports and discouraging imports, notably through the use of tariffs and subsidies. Their claim appears to be supported by Finger and Winters (2002) who reported that the average depth of tariff reduction by developing countries was substantially greater than that agreed to by high-income countries. In addition, developing countries had to take on costly commitments such as those embodied in the sanitary and phytosanitary standards (also called the SPS agreement: the World Trade Organization set limits on member-states' policies relating to food safety [bacterial contaminants, pesticides, inspection, and labeling] as well as animal and plant health [phytosanitary] as related to imported pests and diseases) and Trade-Related Aspects of Intellectual Property Rights agreements (Finger and Schuler 2001).

Postadjustment Changes

The success or otherwise of the reform program has been weighed by various economists and other academics. Fik (1999, pp. 20–21) noted that there is very minimal available evidence to back the success of this program. Fik buttressed his stance on the basis that the development of a production network that was characterized by an expansion or strengthening of the intraformal sectoral linkage system was nonexistent. There is some evidence that IMF stabilization programs do have a positive impact on the balance of payments and current account. However, evidence for reductions in inflation and encouragement of growth is rather limited and debatable—there are some serious problems in measuring the empirical success of IMF programs. It is extremely difficult to gauge the counterfactual, what would have been the outcome if the IMF program had not been implemented at all. Indeed, the "before and after" evidence of success in the balance of payments is weaker than calculations of success relative to the counterfactual. (Bird, 2001)

Unlike the preadjustment era, postadjustment developments tend to indicate that the most important and significant change was associated with the intraformal sectoral linkage system. A classic case is the derailment of the traditional forward linkage between sawmills and downstream processors within the formal sector, which as a matter of fact is fundamental to the production network in any regional development equation (Fik, 1999, pp. 20–21). As reported by Barker, Boateng, and Moreno (1991, p. 1), these private entrepreneurs were incapable of supplying local manufacturers with wood products, and at the same time, the manufacturers were unable to keep up with the export demand in terms of quality and/or quantity for foreign markets. This situation led to the emergence of an intensive formal-informal sectoral linkage system as indicated by Owusu (2001). Prices for the reprocessed "off-cuts" and rejected lumber previously purchased from the sawmills plummeted due to the fact that there was a shift of lumber sourcing for secondary-stage processing from the formal sector (which, by the way, was favored by the government) to the informal sector. As a result, firms within the formal sector, such as those engaged in the manufacture of furniture and other accessories, had no option but to purchase low-grade material from the informal market rather than directly from the sawmills within the formal sector, which, although relatively more expensive, guaranteed better quality. This shift appears to be significant considering the fact that the informal sector attracted little or no attention from the government (UN/ECA, 1986, p. 3; World Bank,

1989, p. 135) as in the allocation of the Structural Adjustment Program–related production incentives. Revenue from the export of lumber and lumber products showed a steady increase from US$21 million in 1984 (Owusu, 1998b, p. 427) to US$171 million in 1998 (2000, p. 45).

Owusu (1998b) demonstrated that local currency devaluation under the adjustment program placed tremendous pressure on Structural Adjustment Program–beneficiary sawmills to increase output for the international market as a viable means of amortizing their debts in the local currency. The equivalent of the Sector Adjustment Loans in the local currency, the *cedi*, had systematically and significantly increased as a result of the fall in the value of the local currency and, with an increase in interest rates, bank lending rates for the manufacturing and export sectors increased from 20 percent in 1984 to 39 percent in 1993 (CBS, 1983; SS, 1995) to 47 percent from 1995 to 1997 (SS, 1997). This scenario explains in part why the sawmills were very hesitant to sell lumber to the downstream processors, those engaged in furniture and fixtures production, at prices below the prevailing US dollar exchange rate or in a transaction that had to do with the local currency. As a result, small-scale furniture firms that produced for the domestic market and enjoyed strong linkages with the construction sector had access to and purchased lumber inputs from the informal sector just to stay afloat. Akuaba Limited, one of the elite furniture and furniture accessories production firms in Ghana, represents a classic case of the postadjustment disruption of the traditional intrasectoral linkage between sawmills and the formal wood processing groups. Akuaba, which produces for both domestic and foreign markets, benefited from the Sector Adjustment Loan package under the Export Credit Guarantee Department (of the United Kingdom) loan scheme, a reason this firm occupies the top spot on the pecking order of furniture business.

Although it has been several years following the inception of structural reform, this program still remains a hot topic and has become contentious among economists and policy makers, most likely due to its seemingly indelible footprint on the path toward economic recovery. The bone of contention is the overall effect of structural reforms and trade liberalization, and the socioeconomic well-being of countries, especially those of the developing world, with emphasis on household welfare and poverty. Ackah and Morrissey (2005) reported an increase in imports following trade liberalization in a number of sub-Saharan African countries, but this increase was not commensurate with expansion of exports. Instead, exports failed to grow with an increase in trade deficits, bringing the sustainability of the original liberalization into question (Ackah & Morrissey, 2005).

A case in point is access to an increased variety of imported goods that tend to have a comparative advantage over locally produced items on the basis of appearance, function, durability, and sometimes price. Although, this policy might appear to benefit the customer, the economic implications are certainly far reaching for local entrepreneurship (Ackah & Morrissey, 2005). On the flip side, the positive effect of adjustment reforms has been the reduction in the price of imported goods due to the reduction in import restrictions, such as import tariffs and nontariff barriers, which ultimately lower domestic prices of these goods. Furthermore, all things being equal, devaluation of local currency resulted in a general reduction in export prices that led to an increase in export volumes, ultimately boosting domestic output, employment, and external earnings.

Photos

Color:

1. One of the open markets in central Accra. These urban market places often double as shopping precincts and bus terminals.
2. A rural household consisting of a number of units that house the members of the family. In the foreground is a collection of firewood used as the main source of energy for cooking.
3. Southern rural folks at the village borehole, which serves as their source of water for domestic use.
4. A northern Ghana community. Homes built from mud with thatched roofs are typical of this region.
5. A young man in a neighborhood of Accra is seen here transporting a load of farm produce by means of a two-wheeled cart. Most of the male migrants on the streets in Accra offer services this kind of to the vendors.
6. The Buipe field research liaison flanked by two northern women who are mothers of some members of the participants.

Black & White:

7. A closer look at the open market in Accra. The structures in the background are stalls that house the vendors, most of whom sell farm produce and fish.
8. Drawing of a grave by a South African street child.
   Courtesy: Jill Swart, 1990.

B & W Photo 7

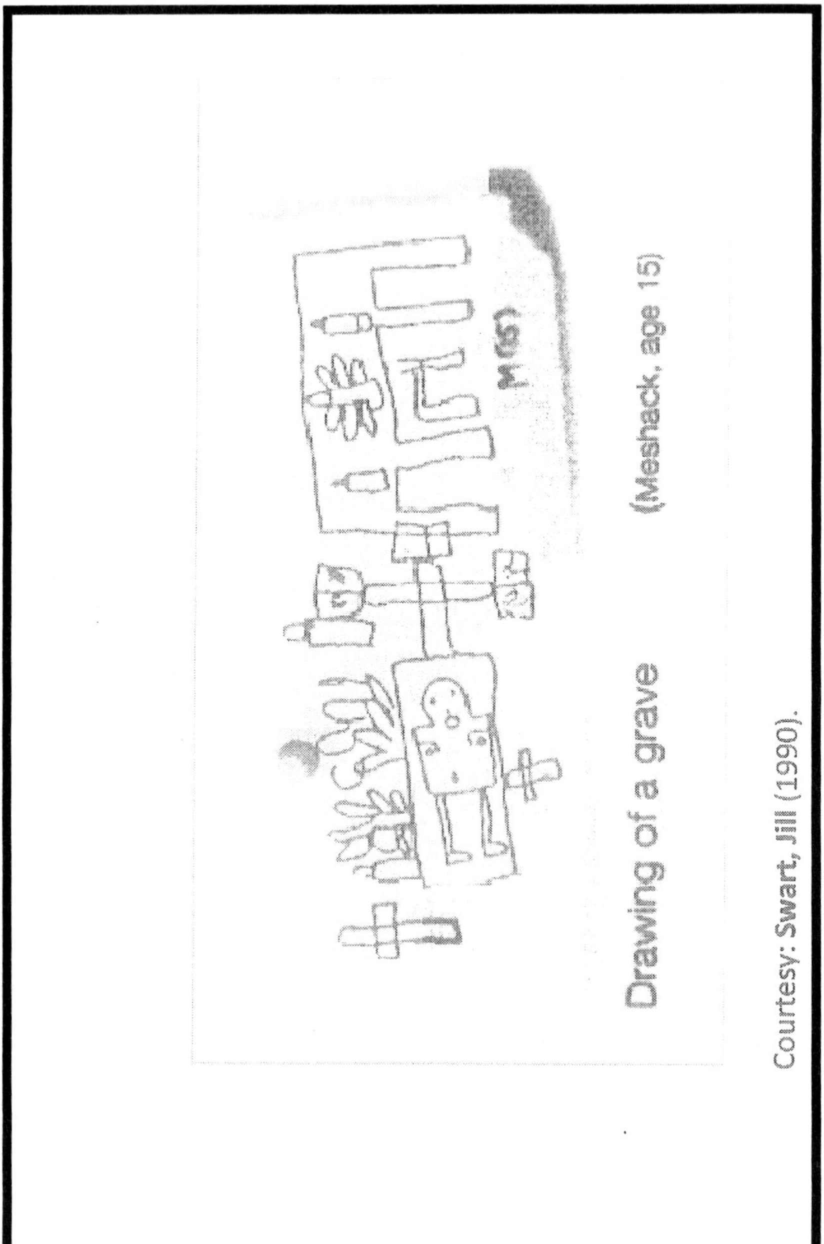
M (15)
Drawing of a grave (Meshack, age 15)
Courtesy: Swart, Jill (1990).

B & W Photo 8

Chapter Six
Methodology and Emerging Themes

Phenomenological methods in combination with symbolic interaction and family systems theory were utilized in the design of the method and data collection. This approach is attractive from a contextual standpoint in an attempt to understand the factors underlying the desire of youth to leave their rural homes for urban streets. I have often asked whether each family system and the given set of guidelines in a given family system within the Ghanaian society have any role to play in the initiation and sustenance of this phenomenon and, if so, to what extent. Additionally, the fact that no family is completely closed or opens suggests that families are permeable, and so there is the potential for interaction across family lines to contribute to this phenomenon in whatever fashion. Allowing the participants to tell their own stories without any limitation or restrictions is necessary to provide a better understanding of the mechanisms that drive their decisions. Do these children see any incentive in enduring the constant exposure to the vast array of challenges on the streets from within their cohort and the general public? Are these decisions driven by their social settings, and are these value perceptions based on their interpretative processes? For researchers to understand and appropriately interpret this trend among street children, it is imperative to critically consider the responses in the face of challenges and interpretation of their street experiences (Ek & Steelman, 1998; Raffaelli et al., 2001; Schaffner, 1999). By so doing, the outcome will be fundamentally influenced by the interpretation of the phenomenon from an emic or insider's perspective.

This study was conducted in three phases: focus groups, interviews, and fieldwork. The focus group phase was conducted in 2003 at the Kaneshie Market within the Accra Metropolitan District in the Greater Accra Region. This site appeared attractive due to the fact it is one of the largest and most intense markets within the metropolis, making it an inviting waterhole for potential street children. In addition, the fact that this market is remote from the Catholic Action for Street Children youth shelter within the district, where part of the study was conducted, provides an added precaution, which reduces the chances of potential duplication of subjects. Sampling was conducted based on accessibility and was completely devoid of coercion or any form of incentive. The focus group consisted of eleven females ranged from twelve to seventeen years, all of whom migrated from the Northern Region of the country. These girls worked at this market as *kayayo*, the local term for people tasked to cart agricultural produce to and from the market, or *kayaboiler*, who are responsible for the daily disposal of garbage from various eateries. Occasionally, these girls will diversify by engaging in other unrelated menial jobs such as dish washing and cleaning at eateries that are mostly run by women within the market. In my interaction with this group, it became apparent that these girls were imbued with enduring resilience, tenacity, great purpose, and unquenchable hope.

The interviews were conducted in 2003 with children who were seeking help from the two NGOs, Catholic Action for Street Children and Tizaa Action Aid, located in the Accra Metropolitan District and Tamale municipality in the Greater Accra and Northern regions of the country respectively. These were street youth who spent a great amount of time on the streets, as a way of life and a means to an end, totally devoid of adult supervision or care. A total of twenty-four street children were interviewed from the months of February to May of 2003 in a one-on-one, in-depth, open-ended format (Berg, 2001, p. 115). This method allowed for better exploration into this understudied subject (Rosenblatt and Fischer, 1993, p. 173). The participants had been on the streets for at least six months, which qualified them for this study in accordance with the guidelines provided by the United Nations Children's Fund of "youth of the street," as one whose ties to family or household is occasional and, at best, tenuous (Mufume, 2000). The interviews were conducted exclusively in the native language of choice for easy and effective communication without any interpretation, as the author is proficient in six native languages. In addition, these interviews were audio recorded, lasting an average of four hours with minimal public intrusion even as they were held in the open shopping precincts.

The field study was conducted in two phases, the first of which was in 1996, which was purely preliminary and involved daily observations with minimal interaction with the children for a three-month period at the Catholic Action for Street Children within the Accra metropolis.

The second phase was conducted in 2003 as a two-week visit to the parents of some of the participants who live at Buipe and the Tamale municipality in the Northern Region. This followed the interview and focus group phase of the definitive phase of the study. The field notes were collated, coded, and subsequently analyzed for emerging themes.

The Ghanaian Street Child

Studies on this phenomenon in Ghana (Beauchemin, 1999) and the African continent (Mufume, 2000) demonstrate rural–urban migration as overwhelmingly responsible for the presence of children on urban streets. In fact, an overwhelming majority of the participants, approximately 97 percent as we will see later in this chapter, migrated from the rural communities of the country. The stories presented by the participants showed strong commonalities in that all the participants are members of large (an average of six siblings) and very low-income families. This trend is not uncommon across the country and is very consistent with the statistics for the Northern Region. As indicated in the preceding chapter, most families, especially in the northern parts of the country, rely on their children for labor, the males assigned to the farms and females tasked to help sell farm produce on the local market. This practice tends to affect the overall grade school, middle school, and high school enrollment, with greater female enrollment occurring at the early stages of education as the males are required to work on the farms at the early stages of their development, compared with the girls who become eligible to work at the market later in their development. Their parents, according to these children, were engaged in subsistence agriculture, fishing, or were simply unemployed—a claim consistent with regional statistics. A subgroup of this cohort was experiencing at least one of the following: single parenthood as a result of divorce, extramarital pregnancy, death, child neglect, or abandonment by the absentee biological parent, a trend strongly supported by the regional demographics outlined in the previous chapter.

It was observed that a subgroup from the Northern Region, largely female, migrated in search of job opportunities such as *kayayo* or sales assistants to sole proprietors. It is commonplace to see clusters of this subgroup within the shopping precincts. It was apparent from the interviews that this group held the view that their presence on the street was temporary and that they planned to return once they achieve their desired goal.

Another subgroup, from rural southern Ghana, indicated that they leave home for a number of reasons, and their presence on the streets is more obvious than the *kayayo* subgroup from Northern Ghana. Unlike the *kayayo* subgroup, this tier is not selective and will offer to undertake any task as long as it brings food and money to them just for the day. It was noted that this subgroup has a greater tendency to seek assistance from agencies and will utilize any opportunity that is made available to them because for them, it was matter of survival. It appeared that this group had abandoned their cause and were not willing to return home, at least not in the near future and so, for now, they called the streets home. It became evident that this subgroup faced greater uncertainty on the streets and were more likely to engage in activities that are proscribed by law.

In addition to this subgroup, there are the second-generation street children, who ranged from infants to ten-year-olds, products of extramarital pregnancies from the two subgroups mentioned above. These children were not as visible; they were occasionally seen with their mothers as they roam the streets and were more often seen at shelters provided by NGOs. Some of this second generation are likely to become street children themselves or are simply sent back to their rural homes. This trend appears to have a lowering effect on the average age of street children within the country by a few units. It is evident from these observations that although these children share a lot in common on the basis of rural–urban flow and their street experiences, essentially there appears to be a significant difference in terms of the goals these children strived to attain.

Table 1 – Demographics for Participants Using the NGO Programs in Tamale

(Note: All rural migrants but within walking distance)

Subject	Age (Years)	Number of Siblings	Father's Occupation	Mother's Occupation	Period on Urban Streets (Months)
Musa	17	3	Deceased	Unemployed	12
Kasim	17	4	Deceased	Seamstress	24
Mohamed	16	6	Peasant	Homemaker	12
Ahmed	16	3	Deceased	Unemployed	24
Yousif	15	6	Deceased	¶	6
Moro	15	5	Unemployed	Unemployed	24
Attu	15	6	Peasant	Peasant	6
Alima	17	7	Peasant	Peasant	36
Azara	16	2	¶	Unemployed	12
Memuna	16	2	Unemployed	¶	6

¶ = Abandoned Family

Table 2 – Demographics for Participants Using the NGO Programs in Accra

(Note: All rural migrants from villages in other regions. *indicates urban origin)

Subject	Age (Years)	Number of Siblings	Father's Occupation	Mother's Occupation	Period on Urban Streets (Months)
Twum	15	1	¶	¶	48
Abukari	17	4	Deceased	Peasant	36
Iliasu	16	8	Deceased	Peasant	72
Atta	17	2	Hawker	Deceased	12
Cudjoe	17	4	¶	¶	8
Dapaa	15	5	¶	Hawker	7
Aminu	17	4	Ranch Help	Homemaker	12
Ekua	17	1	¶	Unemployed	18
Ewura	16	7	¶	Hawker	36
Abena	15	5	Unemployed	Unemployed	36
Ama	15	5	¶	Unemployed	12
Merri	15	8	Peasant	Peasant	12
Adia	16	5	Fisherman	Fishmonger	18
Salamatu	16	7	Fisherman	Fishmonger	8

¶ = Abandoned Family

Table 3 – Demographics for Participants (All Females) at the Accra Kaneshie Market

Subject	Age (Years)	Number of Siblings	Father's Occupation	Mother's Occupation	Period on Urban Streets (Months)
Zenabu	16	7	Fisherman	Fishmonger	22
Zaratu	15	8	Peasant	Homemaker	16
Minatu	16	5	Peasant	Homemaker	18
Rahi	16	4	Peasant	Homemaker	6
Suweba	16	8	Unemployed	Hawker	12
Jamila	13	12	Peasant	Homemaker	17
Dari	15	11	Hawker	Hawker	14
Ayisha	15	2	Peasant	Deceased	7
Fuseina	16	7	Peasant	Homemaker	9
Sadia	12	9	Shoe Repair	Homemaker	11
Munira	14	12	Deceased	Homemaker	13

The Life of the Street Child

Self-Definition

This section will detail the experiences of street life, which will be followed by emerging themes that will help explain the factors that trigger this rural-urban flow.

In their own self-description, it became apparent that these children were very much aware of the public's impression of them and were quick to deflect these thoughts, because the participants constantly reminded me they were in transit and that the street was everything but home. They placed emphasis on the notion that their rural community was home and stated repeatedly that their presence on the streets was a means to an end, and that they will one day say goodbye to the urban streets.

A member of this cohort is Cudjoe, a seventeen-year-old boy at the Catholic Action for Street Children day shelter in Accra, where he made frequent visits following his arrival on the streets eight months ago. Cudjoe attributed his presence on the streets of Accra to child abandonment and was of the conviction that by making it to the city, he would be in a position to provide for his siblings. Below is the interview Cudjoe granted:

Question: How did you become a street kid?
Cudjoe: I am not a street kid; I am just trying to find help here to fulfill my aspirations.
Question: What are your plans for the future?
Cudjoe: I want to become a priest.
Question: Why did you make this choice?
Cudjoe: I did a lot of stealing as a kid as way to stay afloat because my parents abandoned me. I would like to become a priest some day with the belief that the Lord will forgive me. By becoming a priest, I believe I will lead a more responsible life.
Question: Do you think you can achieve any goal under these conditions?
Cudjoe: I am sure I will be lucky enough to get respite someday.

Another member of the cohort is Iliasu, a sixteen-year-old boy, who migrated to Accra from the Northern Region. He has nine other siblings; his father is deceased and his mother, who lives in a village in Northern Ghana, is too poor to adequately provide for them. Iliasu, who wants to acquire a decent education and knows very well he has to work for it, migrated to Accra at the age of ten and, at sixteen, still carts farm produce. At this point, I was of the impression that a child who has spent six years roaming the streets would be willing to call the urban streets "home". Iliasu did not hold that view and was of the hope that the urban streets would serve as a platform on which a decent career would be built. Iliasu's story appeared to provide, once again, another instance of how these children perceive a destination beyond the urban streets. Below is Iliasu's response when asked why he migrated to Accra:

> I came to the city in anticipation of making money to enable me re-enroll in school because my education was terminated following my father's passing. My mother works on the family farm to provide for my siblings and I, and that is how far she is able to go to sustain us. There is barely enough food to feed us all. I felt the need to be in school and acquire formal education. I am eager to return to school, after which I will learn a trade so I can manage my books rather than hire someone, when I own a business venture some day. That is the only way I can help myself, my siblings, and my mother. Now that I am here, there is no room for error because I do not want my kids to end up on urban streets too. I do not want to see my children experience this treacherous life in future, and so I have to learn a trade and return home to can raise a family.

Attu, a sixteen-year-old from the rural Northern Region, offers her version of self-definition. Attu arrived in Tamale, the regional capital, six months ago. Attu indicated she came to Tamale following the example of another girl from her village who had demonstrated some level of success after working in the city through the support of an NGO. Attu was impressed and was of the hope that this trajectory would ultimately transform her dream of becoming a beautician into reality. Attu narrated her life on the streets and underscored the notion that the urban street is a transit point on her march to attaining her desired objective. Below is Attu's rendition:

> **Question**: What are your long-term goals?
> **Attu**: I would like to become a hair stylist.
> **Question**: So, I guess that is the reason you are seeking help?
> **Attu**: Yes.
> **Question**: Will you return to your village after learning a trade?
> **Attu**: No. I will stay in the city and work.

It is evident from this conversation with Attu that some of these youth do not self-describe as children on the streets; instead, they perceive life on the urban streets as a viable pathway by which they are able to reach their financial goals. It became apparent that these children were of the strong view that the urban street is a place that affords hope, opportunity, and ultimate financial success. My interactions with families in two Northern villages, from which many of these children originate, will further reinforce this self-definition. The overwhelming majority were dismissive of the "street kid" brand assigned to their migrant children, spoke about their absence as temporary, and looked forward to a heroic return. Although these families expressed great optimism, they were unambiguous about their wish that the rural environment were a place of opportunity and success. I felt these families had a legitimate reason to respond the way they did. Ali and Fatima are parents who indicated how they miss their daughter who migrated to the urban community six months ago and fervently hoped for success for their daughter. To them, calling the streets home was a remote possibility, and they believed her departure was temporary. "Look at this place, hopelessness is everywhere," were Fatima's words. "These children need to improve their lot, but, unfortunately, there are no opportunities in our community," she added. She went further to indicate her daughter is a very responsible and hard-working child, and believed she would return home, in due course, as a successful girl. Fatima indicated her daughter is modest and would return home as soon as she able to raise just enough money.

Life on Urban Streets

Life on the street is characterized by never-ending, arduous labor under the stifling tropical heat. I observed one subgroup of the street children who worked primarily by manually carting farm produce to and from the market. These children spend most of the day at the very busy markets, such as shown in Figure 1, where customers routinely make bulk purchases. The children are readily available to hand cart the produce for their prospective clients for a paltry sum of money. This kind of service comes in handy in areas of the marketplace that are virtually inaccessible to vehicular traffic. This cohort is usually seen with hand basins, an indication that they are engaged in carting goods when and if the opportunity comes their way. I observed that reservations are not made, and although these children appear to be a conglomerate during the idle periods of the day, this façade disappears instantaneously when business comes their way; these children scramble for the single opportunity that could be available to them by literally jostling each other. There are no defined guidelines in this kind of environment; instead, the rule of survival of the fittest reigns supreme and winner takes all.

Zenabu, who is sixteen years old and migrated from Northern Ghana, is a member of this transportation group at the Kaneshie Market, as shown in Figure 1, who participated in a focus group. At the time of the interview, she had been on the streets of Accra for twenty-two months. Zenabu comes from a family of nine, including her parents who fish and rely solely on the paltry sales they make from the daily catch. Asked what a typical day on the streets looks like, Zenabu said:

> In the early hours of the morning, you hear a rooster crow, and that signals it is time to go to the market. The rooster serves as the alarm clock for us on the streets. We have to wake up at dawn because that is when vendors are beginning to get their goods over

> to the market. We wake up early and walk to the market. It is quite a distance so we set out early and by the time we get to the market it is daybreak. When we get to the market, there are chances that none of us gets hired. In the event that we fail to secure any clients, one will have to go hungry. In situations like this we are on the alert and when a vendor calls for our service, there is fierce competition for this opportunity.

Sixteen-year-old Minatu, who briefed me on the challenges at the job place on the streets, is engaged in transporting market goods and says:

> Sometimes, someone calls for our service, and we literarily run for it. We get there and realize it is heavy stuff in the extreme. Although we are very much aware that we are not structurally built for this kind of function, we make an effort anyway; sometimes one may even stumble and fall with these goods, sustaining long-term injury. This situation is prevalent especially on rainy days. For some of us, our homes may be comfortable because we at least get a little bit of food to eat, but we still have to come here and endure this because it is the only way to get something beyond the meals one gets at home. We do this just out of pure necessity.

Other children expressed sentiments similar to those of the focus group. I met Mohamed in Tamale, the Northern regional capital, who had been on the streets for about one year and relying on menial jobs at the market for survival. Mohamed is a member of a family of nine. His father engages in subsistence agriculture and his mother is a homemaker. Mohamed spends a typical day at the bus terminals, where he will provide services by carting baggage and farm produce to and from the market. Mohamed's story offered me a window of opportunity to appreciate the daily challenges these children face:

> Well, I just hang out here at the bus terminal. . . . This is how it works out here. The trucks carry goods from different parts of the country. On arriving at the terminal, the drivers contract our services to cart these goods into storage, so we hang around and we get hired on daily basis. By so doing, we are able to provide food

> for ourselves, and on a good day we are able to make some savings.

For the child on Ghana's urban streets, going without adequate food is routine as they earn very little for their services and are able to afford food only when and if job opportunities come their way. Zenabu and her colleagues at the Kaneshie Market expressed the situation of the deplorable food security as a major concern—they could go through a night hungry. At one stage in our conversation, Zenabu, who was one of the voluble members of the party, became a bit emotional and asked why such a basic human necessity as food should sometimes elude them and to that extent. It appeared at this point that Zenabu had come to terms with reality, at least temporarily; and in a very melancholic tone and with head slowly moving from side to side, the sixteen-year-old said, "As for hardships . . . our lives here can only be characterized as challenging"; she wiped a tear and continued, "We face great difficulty out here. We experience so much hardship." She continued by saying that "sometimes we roam the streets all day long hoping that one will not go without a meal, but that is highly possible."

Yousif, a fifteen-year-old boy, echoed Zenabu's sentiments: "Life out here is very difficult. If I am lucky, I find food to eat; and if I am not, I do not find anything for the day." Fifteen-year-old Ama described her version of the food situation this way: "Sometimes I scavenge, looking through dumpsters at the market for leftover food." These children indicated that they could not be the least bit fastidious and that they had to content themselves with whatever came their way. Zaratu, who is fifteen years old, indicated that one simply consumes anything to avoid starving rather than wait for tasty or nutritious food that is more likely to elude one. Zaratu went further to indicate that, although the food accessible to them is insipid and of very low nutritional value, they consume it with great delight and speed to avoid having to share with other members of the group.

It became apparent during the discourse that gaining access to food is not the end of the story; shelter just for each night was of equal concern. It was evident from their narratives that life at night was just as fluid and unpredictable as that during the day. Although these children indicated they used the market stalls as shelter, one had to be prepared to change stalls at any given night. There was consensus on the fact that, at night, one was sure of becoming dinner for the thousands of mosquitoes, which increased the chances of contracting malaria. Sleep was constantly interrupted by traffic, not to mention the low temperatures accompanied by gusty winds on rainy nights. Here is how Yousif described this situation: "We deal with a lot of insect bites because we sleep outside. When the rains come, we become drenched, stay awake, and the nights become very long. For me, almost every night offers a different location, and so I keep moving around, from one place to place." However, some members indicated they find permanent shelter through informal arrangements with other veteran members who usually lay claim to some of the stalls. Sixteen-year-old Minatu described one of these sleeping arrangements this way: "I do not know if these structures constructed for rent are real rooms. They are very small and will accommodate about thirty or even forty people at night." Minatu describes what happens when one first signs on for this service:

> When we first arrive here on the streets, front-runners straight away recognize we are new to the system and treat us as such. When it is time to go to bed, we are offered cardboard paper as mats which provide very little comfort as we sleep. Even when it is time to sleep, the room is filled beyond capacity and you will hear someone yell, "Scoot over"; others say "It is too warm in here," and others say "Do not lie too close to me," all in an attempt to find as much comfort possible through the night.

Other sleeping arrangements can take the form of the driveway in front of the store; and these places are usually controlled by the older members, who lay claim and charge the younger children for space. It is typical for these custodians to play the role of sentinels and take turns in resisting any intruder. This is how Akua, who is seventeen years old, puts it: "In our area, we sleep outside in front of the stores; but it is relatively safe because older boys like Vann Dame will keep watch over the place in exchange for money."

Instrumental Crime

I was struck by the level of candor with which these children talked about their life on the streets and their modus operandi to stay afloat. However, these children were quite hesitant to disclose some of the activities that appeared to border on criminal acts. Their stories revealed that a significant number of these street children will engage in activities that are likely to contravene the law, but only when everything legitimate fails to address some of their basic requirements, such as food. These acts, they confided, usually involve stealing farm produce such as bananas, pineapples, and oranges from vendors; picking pockets; inducing public sympathy by crafting and telling very distressing stories in order to get people to offer them money; for the girls, prostitution sometimes was the order of the day. Ama, a fifteen-year-old girl who migrated from rural Ashanti and had been on the streets of Accra for about a year, appeared resigned to her life in a way and communicated with me in a rather mature fashion. It later became clear that Ama had experienced a difficult past, coming from a family of six who were abandoned by their father. He left when Ama was just seven years old. Ama's mother became physically disabled after giving birth to her younger sister, a situation Ama believes was the cause of the abandonment. Ama, who is the second of the six siblings, migrated with her older brother to Accra because their financial circumstance back at the village was unbearable and they felt the need to leave in search of greener pastures. Shortly after Ama arrived in Accra, she met a woman who offered to provide her the support she desperately needed. It turns out that this woman was a prostitute at the Kwame Nkrumah circle, one of the busiest spots in the city of Accra, and in no time Ama began to make money this way. It was abundantly clear in our conversation that Ama was not the least proud of this practice as she narrated her story: "Okay, the truth is, I am not proud of this, but sometimes I earn some money as a prostitute." She talks about wanting to find a more decent approach to making money, but is resigned to this trade that appears to be "the lowest hanging fruit," something Ama did not want disclose to the other children within the Catholic Action for Street Children youth shelter. "I come to this shelter almost on a daily basis, hoping that I will acquire some form of sponsorship for education. . . . I am racing against time and I hope I am able to provide for myself and siblings, and it is my prayer that my mother will live long enough to see this unfold."

It is commonplace in Ghana to find physically and mentally disabled people by the side of urban streets asking for money. Iliasu, who is sixteen years old, and his younger friend indicated they will take advantage of this practice in very trying times to extort the public to enable them to buy food. Iliasu narrated this story when asked to describe a typical day in his life on the street:

> Usually I start my day with keeping my hygiene. I purchase some water to wash my face and to clean my teeth. I then go to the market place in search of job opportunities in order to buy breakfast. Sometimes I do not have any luck with that and become very hungry. Whenever that happens, I go with my friend (the other boy sitting over there) to beg for some money from passers by. My friend is very good at playing the role of a disabled person, acting as if he is blind and I his guide on the streets. We play our roles so well that, some people cannot help but offer us change. That is how we make money to eat. Sometimes when I am lucky to find someone who hires me as a porter, I make money that way too.

These stories appeared to apply to the other children, who indicated that these acts are not routine and do not constitute the primary means by which they are able to survive, but they emphasized that these practices do serve as the last resort in very challenging times. As they narrated their stories, these children were clear about the level of guilt and shame involved, but justified these acts purely on the grounds that they had to survive. While these stories may suggest these children are scoundrels, as they have come to be known by the broader Ghanaian public, the children went further to indicate that their already difficult circumstances have became even worse as the public was quick to assign blame to them for most of the ills of the urban community.

In the Midst of Exploitation and Harassment

Street youth face numerous challenges because they are exposed to and interact with people from all walks of life; but they strongly acknowledge that this situation is inevitable and forms part of their struggle. Many of the stories they narrated to me revealed the level of exploitation by vendors at the marketplace, who often contract their services. During such business encounters, these vendors sometimes fail to fulfill their part of the contract and/or are physically and verbally abusive in the process.

Fifteen-year-old Ayisha, who migrated from Northern Ghana to Accra and who is one of the *kayayo* at the Kaneshie Market, recounted one such encounter with a vendor who sought her service to cart goods:

> After I settled, following my arrival, I remember going out one day with some of my friends to cart farm produce at the market. I did not know how far that market was from the bus terminal and had to rely on my colleagues who knew their way around town. Fortunately, a female vendor hired me to carry her goods to the bus terminal. We had a standard charge of one thousand cedis, the Ghanaian currency [approximately one dollar] but because I could not speak the language of my new environment at that time, I mistakenly responded one hundred cedis when the lady asked in the local language how much I was willing to charge for the service.

Ayisha continued:

> She quickly hired me and I was happy to have been hired. I carried her goods to the terminal and she gave me a one hundred cedi coin

> and I said "No! I don't mean this one; I mean the thousand cedi note, not the hundred cedi coin." She insisted that I agreed to charge one hundred cedis at the beginning and so that is the end of the story and boarded the bus. I could not help but cry and insult her but that was not enough to reverse the situation [laughter from Ayisha]. I was very angry. Clearly she ripped me off on this one, quite frankly. I later complained to my friends and they told me, they have fallen victims themselves many times in the past and this one is not an isolated case. This is something I was going to have to get used to.

From my interactions with the children, I observed that most of the street children try to work extra shifts whenever the opportunity comes their way in order to make a little more money so they can have some savings. The faster they saved up money, the more they drew closer to returning home. For the girls from the Northern Region, buying household items such as utensils and other kitchen items was their ultimate goal because tradition requires girls to procure these items before going into marriage. For most of these girls, learning a trade was second to securing household items. The children build relationships with some of the vendors, and once that trust is established, they give their earnings to these vendors for safekeeping until they are ready to return to their rural homes.

For some girls, their ultimate goal had been achieved, and all the hard work and sacrifices on urban streets finally paid off. A case in point is the example Jamila cited during a focus group discussion at the Kaneshie Market in Accra. Thirteen-year-old Jamila had already been on the streets for seventeen months and looked forward to returning to her home in Northern Ghana. Jamila, who belongs to a polygamous family and has twelve siblings, indicated she needed to save money for her future home because her father, who practices subsistence agriculture, and her mother, a homemaker, were not capable of adequately providing for her. At the market, she met a woman soon after she arrived in whom she came to trust and consider a mother. Jamila set up a trust with this woman and raised enough money over the seventeen-month period she had been in Accra. Jamila realized she had fallen victim to a scam only when the time came for her to purchase items and return home, her dream totally shattered.

Jamila painfully recounted her ordeal as she narrated this story during the interview:

> In some instances, you see someone at the market to whom you accord great respect and in whom you repose trust. It is not safe to have money where we retire for the nights so we often save our money with traders here in this market. When it is time to return our rural home, this person may lie by indicating that the money was stolen, as it happened in my case. We lose twice as much this way because we spend all this much time away from family and lose those savings with nothing to show for the toil. They will normally give us the run around until we give up on them. At that time, we are unable to provide ourselves with one decent meal but have to rally and start all over again. There is no need spending the rest of the time crying over the loss; instead we just have to muster confidence and start all over again.

Zaratu, a fifteen-year-old member of this cohort, reported an even more chilling story: "We risk on a daily basis becoming targets for foul play and violence. We woke up one morning and found one of the children murdered. It was a terrifying scene."

Jamila's sentiments were echoed by other children in this cohort who were seeking support from an NGO. Other times, exploitation came from within the cohort itself, when the older and physically superior members would coerce their younger and physically disadvantaged counterparts into sharing or completely giving their money away, an indication that the older members, for the most part, ruled the streets. Ewura, who is sixteen years old, offered her version of the story: "Well, there are times the stronger boys will harass you for your money. Even when you indicate there is nothing on you, they strip-search to just to be sure one is not faking it." Ewura went further to indicate that one is likely to be raped when these intruders find nothing after conducting the search.

Atta, who is seventeen years old and is physically diminutive compared with the other boys, concurs with Ewura:

> We face a lot of problems from the physically stronger boys. We have to wake up very early in order to find work before these boys come around. Otherwise they take the jobs away from us. We are all in competition for the work, and sometimes the stronger ones tend to use whatever means possible to deprive us of any job opportunity that might comes way.

> **Question**: So you have to compete to get these jobs?
> **Atta**: Oh! Yes.
> **Question**: What about the money you earn?
> **Atta**: Sometimes the money is stolen from us. The older boys bully us and take our money away from us. That is why we come to the shelter to get away from them.

The children did not mention anything about harassment by law enforcement officers, but they bemoaned the lack of protection from the police. Ewura indicated that law enforcement officers hold the impression that these children constitute an underclass with no rights whatsoever. Fifteen-year-old Abena indicated that although law enforcement officers perceive them, especially the boys, as pickpockets and the young girls as people who moonlight as prostitutes, they act within the confines of the law. Sixteen-year-old Mohamed, who lives in Tamale, indicated that the police will not hesitate to make arrests, especially in cases where one is suspected of using marijuana or committing some other offence. Atta summed it all up when he said, "The police do not bother us as long as we stay out of trouble; but in most cases they do not offer us any protection either when we are distressed."

Going Down a Virtual One-Way Street

Prior to my interactions with these children, I often wondered why they do not return to their villages once life on urban streets becomes challenging and the incline becomes more and more intense each passing day. As I began to interact with these children and listened to their stories, it became apparent that these children assigned great meaning to their presence on the streets, notwithstanding the crushing poverty and the dangers that loomed. For them, they had gone down a one-way street, and returning home was not an option, at least not in the near future.

When sixteen-year-old Zenabu was asked why she will not return home, she responded, "It is to protect oneself from the shame." Zaratu, who is fifteen years old, presented her dilemma this way:

> It is very disgraceful when one returns home with virtually nothing in hand. It is considered that the individual failed to work hard enough. There are instances where some of the girls will rather resort to prostitution to make more money before going back to the village and then indicate they got all the money from working as *kayayo*. . . . Yes, because the entire village has great expectations and so if one returns without anything in hand, it becomes a disgrace to the family. The family takes great pride in the success of its members, and so one will have to do everything to generate something before returning home.

Zaratu's story may provide an explanation, at least in part, why it becomes very difficult for some of these children to return home, even when the conditions on urban streets are so challenging.

Another member of the cohort, sixteen-year-old Rahi, indicated that the only time one has no option but to make an untimely return home is when one's health is compromised, and that is totally acceptable to the rural community. This is how Rahi put it:

> When one of us is ill, all of us, the *kayayo* in this market, make contributions and have the person seek medical attention in the city or sent back home, a decision that depends heavily on the severity of the condition. If this condition is one that appears to be life threatening, the individual is sent back to the rural family. Illness is

> excused and not stigmatized as we do not have any control over situations of this nature.

The above perceptions were shared by street children from other cohorts who indicated they migrated much to the displeasure of their parents, but believed that, like the biblical story of the prodigal son, they will receive a joyous welcome if they chose to return home any day.

Why They Migrate

Several studies have demonstrated that the determinants of migration can vary within and between countries depending on differences in socioeconomic, demographic, and cultural profiles. Factors such as high unemployment rates, low income levels, and unequal distribution infrastructure such as schooling and poor housing are some of the factors that have been identified as major determinants of rural–urban flow (Bilsborrow et al., 1987; Kadioglu, 1994; Nabi, 1992; Sekhar, 1993; Yadava, 1988; CUS, 1990). Although factors such as the characteristics of migrants and family background may be considered relatively less preponderant, these may represent the final pieces needed to complete the puzzle. So far, age appears to be the most uniformly applicable migration pattern in both the developing and the more economically advanced countries. Also, the institution of family as it relates to gender roles, division of labor, traditional values, and customs and belief systems can have far-reaching consequences on the lives of young people. Therefore, it is imperative to consider the characteristic(s) of migrant households and their environs as potential covariates or predictors in the evaluation of rural–urban flow within a given country or region.

This section will be devoted to detailing how ecological, family, and cultural factors play on the dynamics of this migratory pattern within Ghanaian society. Ecological influence relates to the distinct disparity in terms of infrastructural development between the rural and urban communities, which is prevalent in developing countries like Ghana. Ecological factors have been shown to be a strong driving force for rural–urban migration among youth, due, in part, to failing economies in developing countries, which do very little to provide adequate social capital (Assibey-Mensah, 1998; Fentimen & Hall, 1999; Quist, 2001). There is also the other dimension where the rural youth hold perceptions of the urban area as a sanctuary lush with unlimited job opportunities (Mufume, 2000; Little, 1966). As long as there is that infrastructural differential between the rural and urban communities, ecology will play a significant role in the sequestration of these children on the streets, who will not see any incentive in returning to their rural homes even when the incline gets more and more intense.

The difference in perception of the rural and urban economies is not limited to the rural youth. It permeates almost every age group in almost every rural community across the country. It is generally thought that discipline and hard work in urban areas automatically guarantee financial success. Migrant children become disillusioned following their arrival, as they encounter the very insalubrious and potentially stifling urban conditions, but at that point they realize they have walked down a one-way street and the journey back home appears to be almost impossible. The children do not want to be branded a failure by the rural folk, and so the option of returning home is off the table. They are ultimately faced with a reality check, which provides two options: you either swim as the waves mount, or sink.

Rural Ecology as a Push Factor

Although the rural community lacks the opportunities the youth will need to develop their talents, the goal-oriented instinct of this age group is firmly in place. The deplorable and substandard educational infrastructure in most Ghanaian villages (Beauchemin, 1999) is very obvious. This rural-urban disparity in infrastructure is perceived either through their peers or other travelers to the rural community (Little, 1966), or most recently through programs that are aired on the few television sets that happen to be available in some of the rural homes. These programs, especially the advertisements, tend to entice children with the glitz of the urban communities, the unintended consequence of the rural electrification projects that were initiated in the late 1980s (Beauchemin, 1999).

It was somewhat unsurprising during the interviews when the participants were quick to give their own critique of the minimal level of attention their communities enjoy from the government of Ghana in terms of schools and lack of other facilities. To some of them, enrolling in the village school provided nothing more than a placebo effect, and they rather looked far beyond the perimeters of the rural community in seeking to craft a better future.

Ekua, a seventeen-year-old girl from a village in southern Ghana, indicated that she had dropped out of school and migrated to Accra, which she thought would afford her better opportunities. Ekua was dismissive of the rural educational system and referred to it as nothing but a facade. She was of the view that rural education lacked the capability to provide the fulfillment for which it is intended, and so thought it was a complete waste of time.

Ekua stated quite emphatically, "Well, enrolling in a village school was just a waste of time because those who graduated from these schools and the rest of the community are indistinguishable in terms of their knowledge base." Ekua went further to indicate that these graduates fail to advance and end up on the farms just like the rest of the rural community. Other members of the cohort who migrated from northern Ghana shared pretty much the same concerns as Ekua. In my interview with Abukari, a seventeen-year-old boy who migrated from rural northern Ghana to Accra, he cited the lack of employment opportunities in the rural community. Abukari, who had been on the streets of Accra approximately three years at the time of the interview, cited the deplorable economic conditions in his rural community as the reason to migrate. His family engaged in subsistence agriculture with access to very limited land. Here is what Abukari had to say in the interview he granted:

Question: Why did you decide to leave your village for Accra, such an intense environment?

Abukari: Okay, I did not have anything to do for a living back home and so I decided to come to Accra in search of a job. Shortly after I arrived, I worked by carting farm produce at the marketplace. As time went by, I began to interact with some the members of the cohort more and more, and they recommended this shelter. Since then, I have been working at the market and only retreat to this shelter just to get some respite from the busy market climate.

Question: So did you not like any of the job opportunities, such as subsistence agriculture back home, or none of these were appealing to you?

Abukari: Okay, the only thing I could do was to go and work on the farm, but that is not something I am interested in doing the rest of my life, as it is just enough to provide food for the family. I want to acquire some other skill, which, hopefully, will afford me better and sustainable financial security.

Question: What makes you think being in this environment several miles away from home is the more viable pathway?

Abukari: Although I face an array of challenges on these streets, at least I am able to make some money to feed myself and occasionally remit to my family back home. There was no way I could achieve this back home, even if I worked twice as hard. At home, we have access to nothing more than a small piece of land, enough to feed the family and that is it.

Alima, a seventeen-year-old girl from a village in northern Ghana who currently lives in Tamale, indicated she was eager to work but the village setting lacked the resources necessary to establish and sustain jobs, so she felt that migrating to the city was inevitable. Alima said that she had the motivation to work for a living, but there was nothing available to her in the village.

These views were not limited to the other migrant children; some parents shared the same opinions when I had the opportunity to interact with them. Karim is a father of six, whose oldest daughter left home for Accra in search of opportunities. Karim lives with his wife Faiza in a house built from mud with a thatched roof, which are very often vulnerable to the slightest of wind gusts. Karim had just returned from his farm. In the yard was a small area that serves as the kitchen and was usable only on non-rainy days. I spent a few hours talking to the couple about their daughter who left for Accra some eight months ago. Karim indicated it was a decision no responsible parent would ever want to make, fearing the worst, but acknowledged that she left under difficult circumstances, and inevitably so.

Below is Karim's take on this issue:

> These kids look around and there is really nothing available to them by way of substantive job opportunities. The young ones leave the village in droves for the cities, and so the village gets more and more deserted each passing day. Realistically, I do not want my apprehension to stop my daughter from pursuing avenues that will help carve a brighter future for her. Look at me in the eyes; do I look like a lazy man? Look at all the scars I have sustained from my years of manually toiling just to provide the very basics for my family. There are times when the harvest is so bad due to inadequate rainfall or invasion of locusts, and we toil in vain. Of course these young kids have a legitimate reason to not want this to be their way of life. I do not blame them the least for wanting to leave for the cities. There is nothing available to them in this community.

Karim then added:

> We let our children go, not because we are irresponsible parents, but because we want the best for them. This place is unfriendly and although life in the city is difficult, these kids who work hard are able to find a little money in the city, and that improves their life. My neighbor's daughter just returned and is currently married. But for the fact that she went to Accra, she would not be able to make all the purchases for her traditional wedding. Life here in this community gets more hopeless each passing day.

From Karim's perspective, the decision to migrate appears to involve both the migrant child and parents, with a traditional undertone as suggested by Melson (1995).

Perception of Urban Ecology as a Pull Factor

The apparent strong inverse relation between the perception of the rural community's lack of adequate infrastructure and opportunities versus that of the urban community (Little, 1957) is consistent with Karim's mindset reflected in his narrative during my conversation with him. Karim's perception appears to hold true for most of the children who migrate to the cities in search of jobs. In fact, an overwhelming majority of the participants, thirty-one out of the thirty-five youth participants, stated that they chose to move to the city in search of education as the first step to attaining a career and/or outright financial opportunity. Seventeen-year-old Ekua left rural southern Ghana and had been living on the streets of Accra for about eighteen months. Asked why she decided to migrate to the city, Ekua responded:

> I thought I could secure a job, work there for a few months, and earn just enough money to enable me train as a hair stylist here in the city. I realized from the beginning that this was my passion, and so I came up with this plan to migrate to the city and work to raise enough money. My friend indicated to me about how much I could earn working here in the city, and so I decided to give it a shot.

Abena, a fifteen-year-old girl who hails from the rural south, expressed the desire to secure a job opportunity in the city and had this to say: "One of my friends recommended to me that moving to the city will open doors of opportunities, and so I made this move with the hope of improving my life." Zaratu, from the rural north of the country, offered her account, in which she indicated it has been an epic journey and that she and her colleagues decided to migrate to another city, but in the process had a change of mind because she heard Accra was the waterhole from which they could drink unlimited.

So even though the rural and urban communities appeared to contrast each other in the eyes of the unsuspecting migrant youth in terms of opportunities, these push and pull factors appear to work so effectively in unison, providing maximum momentum so powerful that no amount of force is enough to reverse this process of this rural–urban flow. On reaching their destination, the perception of better opportunities in the urban areas soon becomes a mirage, leaving these disillusioned children with no option but to plough through the storm head on, with enduring hope and perseverance. When asked what his expectations of the city were prior to his arrival, fifteen-year-old Moro, who had been living on the streets for two years, indicated he did not anticipate this level of adversity associated with the streets. Sixteen-year-old Zenabu had this to say:

> Some of us come out here with the goal of making money. Once we arrive and realize that life out here is so challenging, returning home becomes a very difficult thing to do. It is very difficult to raise the money we anticipated here on the streets, but asking for money from our families back is not an option, finding ourselves entangled in a complex web with very little chance of extrication.

Family Influence and Disruption

Proper maintenance of the family unit, in this case father, mother, and children, is often considered crucial to the protection, emotional stability, and overall well-being of the developing individual. Children often times become physically detached from their parents as a result of family poverty and/or disruption of the family unit.

The demographics of the Northern and Greater Accra regions, as well as the narratives of the children outlined in the preceding sections of this volume, provide a vivid snapshot of the extent to which family poverty and disruption act as a driving force. There is no doubt that factors such as the size of each household, low literacy rates, poor rural employment opportunities, low rural income, and unforeseen events such as divorce, abandonment, or death of one or both parents will trigger this migratory pattern, often times acting in combination.

It was evident in this study that an overwhelming majority of the participants came from extremely poor rural homes, with just one participant identified as a member of an urban poor family. As indicated by the tables in the preceding chapter, it more likely to have one or both parents of these children engaged in subsistence agriculture or other menial jobs, simply unemployed, having abandoned the family, or deceased. What was more striking in these interviews was the sense of urgency most of the participants attached to the need to leave their rural homes for urban streets in anticipation of job opportunities, which unfortunately are virtually nonexistent in the distressed economy of the country. These children firmly believed that migrating to the urban area was the only viable option to push back the crushing rural poverty.

The story of Musa, a seventeen-year-old living in Northern Ghana, is a case in point. Musa has been on the streets of Tamale for almost a year, seeking assistance from an NGO with the hope of becoming an auto mechanic. Musa's mother is an unemployed widow and has three other children to support. At this tender age, Musa appeared to have developed a profound sense of responsibility to find ways for rescuing the entire family because he was concerned about the chances of his family surviving under the weight of such crushing poverty. Here is Musa's account during the interview:

> I do not make enough money to help them, and that worries me a lot. When I wake up at night, all I do is worry about my mother and my siblings. I think about how they will make it through the day, and I do not have enough to feed myself either. I feel that, being the oldest of my siblings, I have to work extra hard in order to support the rest.

Asked what his plans are for the future as far as providing for his family, Musa said:

> I would like to develop a skill that will enable me support my family in future. Other children at my age have made it through to high school, an opportunity I did not have, but I am determined to learn a trade so I am able to fit with my peers someday. I have to find something to do. I am thinking that if I raise enough money, I

> will start my own business as an auto mechanic here at the market and build a future for myself and my family. I need a trade that will make me eligible for employment. Having a skill will provide a better future for the entire family.

Musa's case was not an isolated one, and many of his colleagues, during my interactions with the cohort both in the Northern and Greater Accra regions, shared Musa's story. Abukari, the seventeen-year-old boy mentioned in the earlier section, gave an account similar to Musa's story. I engaged Abukari in a lengthy conversation about his life experiences, and whenever we discussed his family, he appeared very distraught. Abukari, who left his rural home in northern Ghana for Accra, was hardly in touch with his widowed mother and his four siblings. Abukari's family engaged in subsistence agriculture on a very small piece of land as the only source of food and money. Although working to help load baggage at one of the bus terminals within the city provided minimal reward, Abukari was of the opinion that the benefits outweigh those of the rural home. Asked the reason he was working to earn and save the money he received loading baggage onto buses, Abukari responded:

> I am doing the best I can to save enough money to be able to remit to my mother. I have remitted to my family back in the past months and even bought clothes for my younger brother. These days, I make very little money and I am unable to make remittances as I used to in the past, and that is a concern.

These sentiments about the need to provide financial support for families back in the village were not limited to boys within this cohort. Some of the female participants made the same argument. During my conversation with fifteen-year-old Ama, she indicated to me that she had at times resigned herself to work as a prostitute in Accra. When I asked why she had not chosen to return home to her family, instead staying and wallowing daily in this treacherous environment, Ama responded, "I want to be able to raise money to enable me to buy household items for my widowed mother and siblings when I return to the village."

Besides feeling the need to rescue their families from poverty, to other members of the cohort it was just a way to escape the never-ending indigence of the rural community. Moro, a fifteen-year-old boy from northern Ghana, told me, "I did not anticipate that I would one day end up roaming the streets of a city. However, when I was told that children could work for food at the marketplaces in the city, I decided to explore this avenue." Moro continued as he became somber, "My parents are still alive, but they are unable to provide for us; my dad is so poor and physically challenged that all he can do is go out and glean off the surrounding fields for food." This account was echoed by seventeen-year-old Alima, who hails from northern Ghana. Asked about the quality of her rural life prior to coming to the urban community, she responded, "My family was incapable of providing three square meals a day." She went on to indicate that her life on the urban streets, though unsavory, is relatively better compared to life back home. "At least I am able to secure menial jobs on a daily basis and by so doing, I am able to provide the basics for myself." It is clear from Alima's response that for some of the children, the streets provided a ray of hope and security relative to their rural communities.

The statistics outlined in the previous sections of this book are a testament to the unbalanced infrastructure between the Ghanaian rural and urban communities, hence this migratory pattern. What is more striking is the fact that some of these migrants do not even get the opportunity to utilize the few resources available to rural folk because in some cases, some of these children are recruited to provide support for physically challenged parents. Mohamed, a sixteen-year-old from northern Ghana, gave his perspective on this situation:

> Okay . . . you know, I went to school for a short period, but you know it is all about the money. These days, I barely make enough

> money and so my family cannot afford the school fees to keep me in school, so I dropped out. I joined my parents on the family farm, but as you may be aware, that will not guarantee me a sound future, and so I decided to leave the village, hoping the urban community would provide me better opportunities.

Zaratu, a fifteen-year-old who lives in the southern part of the country, shared her story. When asked whether she had ever enrolled in a village school, she responded with a smile and with these words:

> School? Are you kidding me? Who has money to provide formal education for nine children? Definitely not my family. My parents are unable to afford to put even one kid through school, not to mention nine children. My parents' income is just enough to provide food, shelter, and clothing for the family.

To these children, formal education is a privilege, not a right, and is reserved for parents who are able to provide for their children.

Family disruption as a result of unforeseen factors such as divorce, abandonment, or death was common to the narratives of these children. In most traditional Ghanaian settings, the father represents the head of the household and with this comes the responsibly of solely providing financial and emotional support for the household. Therefore, it is anticipated that the situation becomes even more hopeless for families in which the woman has to assume the role of lone parent in the event of death, divorce, or child abandonment. The male parent is more likely to abdicate, especially in a culture such as that of Ghana, where the average household income is next to nothing and social welfare systems very fragile. The resulting gender imbalance and lack of economic opportunity in the rural community places an even greater constraint on the child, compelling these young individuals to contribute financially to the family income. The timing of death, divorce, or abandonment; the reasons for divorce or abandonment; the level of conflict; and the gender of the custodial parent are core parameters in determining the extent to which the child plays a support role within the family.

In fact, timing appeared to be common to the participants in that, irrespective of whether it was the death of the male figure, divorce, or parental abandonment, these events occurred before these children reached their teenage years. Musa, the seventeen-year-old boy mentioned in the early part of this section, puts the loss of his father and the challenges secondary to this event in perspective:

> I was finding everything very difficult. Before my father died he took care of everything, but after he died it became very difficult. You know how it is, when he died some people tried to help us, but when you depend on someone else almost all the time, they are easily irritated. When my father passed away, I was asked to live with my uncle who was expected to provide for me and was overwhelmed because he also had his own children to support. As a result, my uncle was unable to provide formal education and instead had me stay home and assist him in his business. In this way, I contributed economically to my uncle's family and my future became more and more uncertain, as the days went by. I then decided to go to the city where I could secure a job and begin to craft my own future and that of my siblings.

Below is the account by Abukari, a seventeen-year-old who migrated to Accra from northern Ghana and who has been mentioned in the previous sections of this chapter, regarding his father's passing:

> Okay, I was enrolled in school full time until my father passed away. I had the desire to continue to enroll, but that was not possible because there was nobody to provide me with financial assistance, and so I had to withdraw and have been idle ever since. I believe I have immense potential that will go untapped if I continue to spend my time on the farm, and so I decided to change course.

Sixteen-year-old Ahmed, who lost his father a few years ago, was quick to provide his version. Asked about his mother, here is what Ahmed had to say:

> When my father passed away, all the kids were sent out on fosterage with my aunts because my mother could not provide support for every one of us. My mother had to move in with her brother. I was supposed to join my mother but instead chose to move into the city in anticipation of better opportunities. I came here and started to work as a shoeshine boy as a way to earn money.

Unlike Musa, Abukari, and Ahmed, some participants reported that their fathers either divorced or left the village in search of jobs in the cities and never returned. The fact that most of the male participants experienced the passing of the male figure and are on the streets is consistent with Ghanaian customs and traditions, where the eldest boy is considered second in command next to the father within the family unit. With such a structure in place, the boys see the need to assume the support role the father played prior to his passing, as early as the teenage years.

It is a rare situation that the mother abdicates in financially difficult times. Yousif, a fifteen-year-old boy, offers an example. Yousif was somber when he spoke about how his mother abandoned the family following his father's death:

> My father worked as a construction worker. We lived in the village until he passed away. Following his passing, my older brothers played the support role, but they had to go to the city in search of better opportunities. My mother, siblings, and I continued to live in the village. . . . She traded in basic items and her earnings were just enough for food for the day. One day she told us that she was going to the city market to sell some items and never returned. . . . Yes. That explains why I had to come here just to stay afloat.

Azara, a sixteen-year-old girl in northern Ghana, indicated her father left the family for the city in search of work and never returned. Azara dropped out of school as a result and decided to leave for the city, leaving behind her siblings and mother. Here is what Azara had to say during the interview:

> I enrolled in the village school but had to drop out after the sixth grade. . . . My mom did not have a stable job at that time and was virtually unemployed, and my dad left the family so I was forced to drop out. My mother could not afford the attendance fees.

On the basis of the above narratives, it is evident that the term "runaway" youth as applied to children who primarily leave home for reasons such as overly restrictive rules or parental drug, alcohol, physical, or sexual abuse becomes a misnomer within the Ghanaian context.

The following final section will focus on the impact traditions and customs, as related to primogeniture, marriage, and fosterage, are considered to have on rural–urban flow within the Ghanaian setting.

Primogeniture

Primogeniture, by definition, is the right by law or custom conferred on the first-born male child to inherit the estate, to the exclusion of younger siblings, following the death of the family patriarch. Primogeniture, by this definition, is practiced in most traditional settings across Ghana. The institution of primogeniture could work in favor of or against the oldest son in some respects. In a situation where the oldest son is in line to inherit a large family business that requires management or professional skills, the parents will invest heavily in their son's formal education. However, with inheritance comes enormous responsibility. On the basis of this, there is the potential to be sequestered, depriving the first-born son of the luxury to be socially mobile as they are required to be home and oversee the family business. In a situation where the family business is nothing more than subsistence agriculture or fishing, which do not require formal education but just basic skills, parents may not see the need to invest very much in formal education. This does not in any way preclude the other siblings from acquiring formal education. Even more striking is where the first-born son is a member of a poor household, a more likely scenario in rural Ghana. In such a situation, the boy is expected to start working from early childhood to support his other siblings as the future patriarch of the family. This explains why primogeniture has become one of the very powerful driving forces in many rural communities within the country, especially in the northern belt.

However, primogeniture, as it affects rural–urban migration, does not act in total isolation but in combination with the huge differential of the distribution of infrastructure between rural and urban Ghana. This infrastructural gap gets even wider between the rural north and urban south with time. First-born males, especially from northern Ghana where the practice of primogeniture is broad, expressed being disproportionately burdened. Unlike the children from the southern belt of the country, whose desire to help their families financially was relatively voluntary as the requirements were not overly stringent, those from the north indicated they had an obligation to fulfill by virtue of the fact that they are second in command and will assume the role of the family patriarch in the event that the father passes away. Living with the reality that one is likely to assume the role of caretaker when his father joins his ancestors in the next world, and knowing that there is virtually no estate that will be passed on, it becomes imperative to start working towards that goal early in childhood, a race against time with very little margin for error. This is even more crucial when the male figure is very old, as is the case in the north, where teenage girls are allowed to be married to their much older male counterparts. To these children, this role is sacred, offers fitting tribute to the father after his passing, and is a matter of urgency, as failure of which will cast the family into disrepute. It therefore came as no surprise to me that these children indicated there was no option but to migrate to the urban community in search of economic opportunity in preparedness for their future.

Sixteen-year-old Mohamed, who migrated to the northern regional capital of Tamale in pursuit of financial support from an NGO to enable him to meet his aspirations, is the oldest son of seven children; the family patriarch, who is a peasant, is the sole breadwinner. It became obvious that Mohamed did not believe that his father's farm alone was a viable source of income capable of providing for the family in the long term. Mohamed was of the opinion that his father had to work twice as hard, and that did not even guarantee food security in the event that the region receives low rainfall or a massive pest invasion, which is highly possible considering the climate within the northern belt. These uncertainties were enough to motivate Mohamed to pursue alternative pathways if the family was to improve their standard of living. While he expressed concern about the family's impoverished situation, it was clear to me that Mohamed was even more deeply concerned about the real possibility of having to assume the driver's seat in the event of the passing of his father. Below is the conversation that ensued:

Question: Why did you decide to leave your village and your family for the city?

Mohamed: Okay, this is how it happened. You know, I already mentioned to you that my parents are full-time peasants. I am the oldest son of the family, and so if I delay crafting a future for myself and being able to take responsibility of providing for the family in the event of my father's passing, it would be twice as difficult to navigate when it is time to sit behind the wheel, and frankly, that will be too little and, a matter of fact, too late.

Question: So you are doing this because of your family?

Mohamed: Yes, my sisters do not have this burden because they are females and would be married off to someone anyway. As the only male sibling, I will become the breadwinner in the event of disease or death of any of our parents, especially the family patriarch. It is therefore my sole responsibility to put the necessary structures in place in readiness.

Aminu, a seventeen-year-old boy from rural northern Ghana who migrated to Accra, offers his version in an interview he granted. Aminu's narrative mirrored that of Mohamed. This is to be anticipated as both of them come from the same region. Aminu's decision to migrate to Accra did not resonate with his parents, who felt strongly that, despite the level of indigence facing the family, relocating was not an option and urged Aminu to rescind his decision and rather invest his time in helping his father who is an employee on a ranch. Aminu, who has four other siblings, was not swayed on the basis that the ranch is not the family business and knowing very well that agriculture, especially in the north, is so fluid that his father could end up losing his job at any time. Therefore, Aminu was of the strong opinion that it was not prudent in the least to put all their eggs in one basket. He did not think that was a sound economic pathway to tread if they were serious about carving a better future for the entire family in the event that his father passes away. This was a pretty strong stance on his part. It was clear from my interaction with Aminu that he did not believe his parents knew the full parameters of his anxiety regarding the role he is likely to play should the family patriarch join his ancestors. As a first step in his pursuit of his dreams, Aminu did the unthinkable by stealing and selling his father's bicycle to purchase a ticket. The next thing his family knew, Aminu was bound for Accra, the beginning of an epic and treacherous pursuit of better opportunities. Aminu responded when I asked about his relationship with his family back home:

> No, my parents are very angry at me for the approach I adopted. They do not understand why I had to steal and sell the bicycle. You know, I figured that if I could leave the village, that increases the family's chance to have one more person as the breadwinner in future. Our current situation is totally unacceptable. I just wish they understood me. I may have taken one of the things my father really cherished and uses, but I think this move, though unacceptable, will yield greater returns in the long run. I could purchase several bicycles for him in future when I learn and practice a trade. I plan to go back home in future and I know they will rally around me when I have a trade and can afford to support the rest of the family.

Seventeen-year-old Atta, one of the members of the cohort from a southern village, was on board with the participants from the north. Atta lost his mother and felt that should his father pass away, it will be his responsibility to provide support for his younger siblings, full time. Atta was unambiguous about the need to prepare for this task well ahead of time. Below is my conversation with Atta:

Question: Did you live with your parents?
Atta: Well, my mother is dead, but my dad was the one who took care of me.
Question: What does your father do in the village?
Atta: He repairs broken radios.
Question: Do you have siblings?
Atta: Yes, I have two other siblings.
Question: Where are you in the birth order?
Atta: I am the oldest of the siblings.
Question: Does this make you feel you have a future central role to play within the family?
Atta: Because I am the oldest, my siblings look up to me as the provider in the waiting. My siblings will definitely expect me to provide for them should our father pass away at any time.

Unlike Mohamed, Atta, and Aminu, some of the male participants were fatherless at the time of the study and had already assumed the responsibility of trying to provide for their families. Ahmed, a frail sixteen-year-old from Northern Ghana and the oldest of four children, lost his father and had to drop out of school. Ahmed's mother is battling a chronic illness and lives in the village. Ahmed had this to share with me:

> Well, I need to work extra hard. I need a lot of support. I am the only one out here in this stormy environment. I anticipate succeeding out here and rescuing my mother and siblings some day. Now that my father is no longer alive, I have to be ready to provide for my siblings; there is no other way. I have to succeed. My mother lives in that village because she is chronically ill. I

> would like to be able to remit to her on a regular basis. It might interest you to know that while we were working on the farm at the village, we had access to limited land, which placed constraints on the family because the harvest was low. I am determined to provide at least more decent food, clothes, and healthcare for my family, especially my ailing mother.

Abukari, a seventeen-year-old northern migrant currently in Accra who lost his father, also expressed the need to play the role of caretaker. Although Abukari is not the oldest of the siblings, he is the first-born son, and that makes him eligible to play this role of caretaker, a form of male primogeniture. Here is what Abukari had to say during the question and answer time:

> **Question**: Do you have any siblings?
> **Abukari**: Yes, four siblings.
> **Question**: Are you the oldest kid?
> **Abukari**: No, but I am the first male.
> **Question**: What do you make of the fact that you are the first male? Why is that important?
> **Abukari**: There is no one else to take up the responsibility of providing for the family but me. I was a toddler when my father passed away. At that time, I could not assume this role, but my family was in anticipation that one day, I would be in a position to lead the family. I became emotional after my father died, and I had the urge to help but lacked the capability. With time, I began to hear from my friends that with hard work, I was bound to succeed here in the city. I thought that by coming here, I could make something for myself and be able to provide for my family. I wanted to learn and practice a trade that would fetch me money, enough to support my family.

What was striking in this segment of question and answer time was the fact the female participants did not share these same feelings expressed by their male counterparts, a clear indication of male primogeniture. Of all the female participants, only two of them expressed the need to help provide for their families, but even in this case, they were the oldest of their all female siblings. Azara, a sixteen-year-old girl from northern Ghana, made this revelation:

> **Question**: Do you have siblings?
> **Azara**: Yes.
> **Question**: How many?
> **Azara**: Two other siblings. We are three sisters.
> **Question**: Are you the youngest? By the way, like you, my siblings are all girls. So we share something in common.
> [Azara smiles on hearing this and indicates she is the eldest of the children.]
> **Question**: Where are the other two?
> **Azara**: They are home.
> **Question**: How did you end up here?
> **Azara**: My mother is currently unemployed and my dad left us to find work in the city, and that was the last we heard of him. He has since not returned, and so my mom and I agreed that I would come to the city to find a job opportunity while she stays home with my younger siblings.

The rest of the female participants were of the opinion that they did not have the responsibility to support their families because they have male siblings who, regardless of their ages, will have to assume that role in the event of the passing the family patriarch. On the basis of this tradition, the female participants indicated there was pressure on them to succeed, but it was not based on primogeniture, at least not when they have brothers. For instance, Memuna, who is a sixteen-year-old girl from northern Ghana and the oldest of the children in her family, responded when asked whether her siblings expected her to provide for them should the family patriarch pass away, "No, they do not look up to me. They are males and by virtue of this, bear responsibility to support the family, including me."

I had the opportunity to interact with one of the parents whose child happens to be one of the participants, Mma Adishetu. She has six children, two of whom migrated to Accra at age fifteen and thirteen years. Mma Adishetu's fifteen-year-old son, Ali, left with his younger sister Zaina for the city, but between these two children, Mma Adishetu emphasized that the primary reasons for leaving for the urban location were different in one respect. She revealed to me that Ali, who is the second-born child but the oldest male child, had to leave because he is "the man of the house," as she prefers to phrase it, indicating he is patriarch-in-waiting and is expected to provide for her and the rest of the family in the event that Baba Zubeiru, her husband, passes away.

Mma Adishetu stated that in the case of Zaina, she left for a different but equally important reason, which was nothing similar to Ali's. Below is Mma Adishetu's thought process as revealed in our interaction:

> Ali is a very responsible child and the most eligible to assume his father's role as the family patriarch. The rest of the kids are females so there is no ambiguity in this case. Being the male among all these women, Ali is the only one who will remain in this household, and all his sisters will be married and very likely relocate somewhere in the region or country with their husbands. My husband did not approve of Ali's decision to migrate, not even for the best of reasons such as wanting to provide for the family in the event that Baba Zubeiru passes away. Maria, my oldest daughter, will soon be married and so Zaina decided to leave and work to prepare for her own traditional wedding in the future. It is absolutely certain that she will be the next in line to be married immediately after Maria's wedding.

It was very clear from this discourse that primogeniture played a very significant cultural role in shaping the decision to migrate, especially among the male migrants from the northern belt.

Marriage as a Cultural Influence

Within the Ghanaian social structure, spousal roles are highly segregated (Van Der Geest, 1976; Clark, 1999). Traditionally, the wife assumes all the domestic chores—mainly pottery, food processing, and childcare, while her husband is exclusively tasked with providing shelter and protection, as well as engaging in subsistence agriculture, fishing, or hunting to ensure there is food for the family. The men occasionally engage in weaving, sculpture, or metallurgy. Where subsistence agriculture is the main economic activity, women assist their husbands on the farms and are in charge of selling part of the harvest on the local market. Women in the coastal regions are tasked to sell the catch their husbands bring home from sea. Generally, within the Ghanaian traditional system, young girls are socially programmed for the role of mother and housewife; and the boys are tasked to assist the head of the family in the area of hunting, fishing, and/or farming (Assimeng, 1999, p. 111).

In rural Ghana, marriage is a revered institution because it affords, to a large extent, the recognition of adulthood among one's own kinsfolk (Goody, 1973, p. 95). In fact, socialization of the young within Ghanaian society has the ultimate goal of assuming a successful marital role, a symbol of maturity and respect (Assimeng, 1999, p. 74). For instance, the traditions and customs of the Gonjas of the Northern Region of Ghana dictate that the woman, and not the man, is responsible for providing the resources necessary to effectively play her role as homemaker because at marriage, no bridewealth or dowry is offered (Goody, 1972, p. 17). With this custom in place, young girls have no option but to begin to prepare for marriage well ahead of time by saving money toward the purchase of household items, such as pots and pans, for their future home (Goody, 1973, p. 69). Such preparations are important for equipping the newly married woman with the tools needed to fulfill her duties as a homemaker; more importantly, it is a sign that the woman is responsible and assigns her marriage great value. Women who are seen as unprepared for this role are disparaged by the prospective parents-in-law and the rest of the community, and more likely to lose the prospective husband.

My interaction with the participants put in context the extent to which traditions and customs related to the institution of marriage within the Ghanaian traditional system impact the phenomenon of rural–urban migration among rural youth. The preceding piece of information demonstrates unambiguously that what primogeniture is to teenage boys, marriage is to teenage girls, especially those who migrate from the northern belt of the country. These girls indicated in the interviews they granted that procuring these household items prenuptially was crucial if they wanted to secure their place in marriage. Hence their desire to migrate to the urban location in search of money, to them, was the only sure and viable pathway.

As indicated in early sections in this volume, it is customary to have teenage girls marry men much older than themselves, even if it is against their will, and this practice is prevalent among the northern tribes. Some authors have attributed this practice to the desire of some of these girls to migrate to urban communities as a preemptive move (Beauchemin, 1999). This claim, adduced by these studies, was corroborated by some of the female participants from the Northern Region.

Seventeen-year-old Alima offered a narrative on this terrifying encounter, and she had no option but to become a fugitive. To Alima, her parents chose the easy route when they were incapable of providing her with formal education, given the limited family resources. Below is Alima's narrative:

> **Question**: So did any of your siblings attain some level of formal education?
> **Alima**: Yes, but only the boys and not the girls.
> **Question**: So what would have happened if you stayed home idle?
> **Alima**: I would be married off to a complete stranger in a heartbeat.
> **Question**: Really? Is this routine or occasional?
> **Alima**: Yes, the girls barely enjoy any formal education because the impression is that they will be married off anyway. My parents think there is no incentive in giving formal education to the girls as all they will do is find a man who is capable of providing financial support, even if the arrangement is against the girl's will. That ends up being a very tough situation

> because then, the man becomes very abusive for the simple reason that I have to depend on him for almost everything.

It appears from Alima's story that her decision to migrate was based purely on a cultural practice she considered potentially crippling and stifling. She would rather endure the sleazy conditions of the urban streets than to be enslaved to a complete stranger. Armed with this perception, Alima indicated, she had to take a preemptive approach and flee before this social tsunami struck. She decided to migrate to the city in anticipation of raising money from menial jobs that would eventually provide some financial platform on which she could build a career.

Sixteen-year-old Zenabu offered her own critique of this practice and indicated she migrated to avoid being married off by her family. Here is what Zenabu had to say when I interviewed her:

> **Question**: Zenabu, tell me why you decided to migrate.
>
> **Zenabu**: I had friends who came here in search of job opportunities. Anyway, my sister, who is a year older than me, just got married to a much older man she had never met, and I knew that it was my turn to go, and it was just a matter of when, not if. I did not want to be married to a man twice my age and who may even have other wives. I know how miserable it is to be in such a marriage and not even have utensils to feed my family and items to bathe a baby. I decided after my sister was married that I was not going to be like her, so I secretly saved money and joined a group of girls who were coming here . . . and they brought me along. My mom was the only one who was privy to this idea.
>
> **Question**: So, your mother approved of the idea?
>
> **Zenabu**: Yes, she has seen how my sister faced numerous challenges in her marriage. My father would have been very mad at her if he knew that my mother was aware of about my plans to leave.

Minatu, a sixteen-year-old from the north, when asked what she expected in the city before she left home, brought up her future role as a married woman with this response:

> I never went to school and there is not much I can do in my village for money. . . . I did not want to be married off with little or no money so I decided to migrate as the others have done. There are drivers who drive to the city, and they secretly help us with transportation. We get to come here and they direct us where the other girls from our village reside. The driving force was my desire to become a seamstress. I am interested in this field so that when I am married, I will not have to be dependent on my husband for everything. I will be self-supporting at least to some extent. I want a regular source of income. I came here to work and buy a sewing machine. I was not enrolled in school at some point, and instead spent all the time helping on the farm.

The effect of the entrenched custom of marriage, in most of rural Ghana, on this migratory pattern was very obvious within this cohort, especially for the girls from the Northern Region of the country as shown by the preceding interviews. These girls looked forward to their future marital role with intense expectation. They savored the opportunity to be married someday and raise their children, but this will come at a cost: they must raise money to procure an assortment of basic household items in preparation for their roles ahead as homemakers and, of course, mothers. Inevitably, these girls thought the pathway to acquiring the much-needed purchasing power would not be easy, and the urban location was the preferred staging ground as their rural economies lacked the structures to generate capital.

Fifteen-year-old Zaratu, who migrated from a village in northern Ghana, narrated her story. Zaratu indicated she is one of nine siblings, and her family relies heavily on subsistence agriculture. At fifteen, Zaratu is very close to entering the institution of marriage and, as mentioned in the earlier sections of this book, teenage girls, especially within the confines of the traditions of northern

Ghana, are already eligible for marriage. Zaratu could see that coming. She was all poised to prepare adequately and, for her, it is a race against time. So she decided to migrate to Accra as the first step on her march to motherhood. Zaratu was all fired up and excited, knowing she will surely reach the Promised Land one day, and cannot wait to play this out. At one point Zaratu appeared to be day-dreaming as she described her role as a new bride and subsequently a mother, though not knowing much of the man to whom she has been betrothed. She clearly indicated that the need to get set for marriage was the primary reason for leaving her rural home. Zaratu went further to indicate that the need to migrate in search of opportunities was even more urgent because of the stigma that she risks in the village setting if she went into her marriage unprepared. Here is what Zaratu had to say during the interview:

> **Zaratu**: You know what forces bring us out here? It is all about marriage.
>
> **Question**: Marriage?
>
> **Zaratu**: Yes marriage, the requirements of marriage. Presently, when one is ready to enter this institution, one has to acquire all the necessary utensils and other household items to set up the home. My parents are too poor to provide these things to prepare me for marriage. Unfortunately, when I disclosed my plan to go to the city and work for the money, it did not go well with them. So I had no option but to leave, knowing they will relent with time and rally around me when I return with some cash.
>
> **Question**: Okay, that makes sense. So what happens to those who go into marriage without these items you just mentioned?
>
> **Zaratu**: It becomes an insult and a disgrace. It labels one as a poor person, and it is stigmatizing.
>
> **Question**: Is it possible to come across these household goods without leaving the village?
>
> **Zaratu**: No. It is not possible.
>
> **Question**: Why?
>
> **Zaratu**: There are no jobs available to make that possible.

Mma Adishetu, who earlier talked about her thirteen-year-old daughter Zaina's migration to the city, spoke about preparations for marriage as a reason for migrating. She was in favor of her daughter's decision to migrate and hoped she would stay focused on the job, in order for her to secure a sound financial base in preparation for her inevitable role as a future bride. I asked her why she thought it was a good idea that Zaina had to leave for the city, and here is her response:

> Once Zaina turned thirteen, I began to worry about her future. Maria [her older sister] is about to get married, and I feel very comfortable and optimistic. This is so because Maria left to join her peers to work at the market in Accra and by so doing she was able to purchase her traditional clothing that she will need to wear as a married woman as well as other items. She is well prepared with all the utensils and other household items she will need, and I will be a proud mother when she is given into marriage. Zaina is equally capable of working. She will go empty handed to her marital home, if she fails to migrate. That is not an option. I was fortunate to be married at a time when it took very little to set up our home. Currently, kids need many more items. If Zaina went on to marry with an empty pair of hands, it would be a complete disaster and all of us will wallow in disgrace. God forbid that should ever happen. I am praying for Zaina's success and confident she will secure all the items she needs before the wedding.

From these preceding segments, it is without a shadow of doubt that these young girls demonstrate profound fidelity to the customs and traditions of their rural community and will go extreme lengths to fulfill every expectation. From these narratives, these girls believe that roaming urban streets in pursuit of their dreams is inevitably a way of life, at least in the short term, all in fulfillment of the dictates of the customs and traditions that have been handed down from generation to generation, inscribed boldly on lead.

Influence of Fosterage

Child fostering—which entails the delegation of parental obligations to persons, usually external family members or friends, other than the biological parents for an extended period of time—is a common practice in sub-Saharan Africa (Mufume, 2000; Eloundou-Enyegue & Stokes, 2002)

Available anthropological and sociological literature has provided some insights into this practice, not all of which have been confirmed by quantitative studies (Goody, 1982; Dupire, 1988; Lallemand, 1976, 1980, 1993, 1994; Etienne, 1979; Savané, 1994; Jonckers, 1997). Fostering represents an expression of persistent traditional kinship and solidarity and is instrumental in creating or reinforcing family ties between individuals or social groups in a given cultural setting. Also, this practice affords an element in a system of exchanges between residential units within the kinship group. Large-scale collection of reliable demographic data in sub-Saharan African countries had to wait until political independence. Early population censuses showed the extent of fosterage practices in a number of countries, such as Ghana, Liberia, Sierra Leone, Nigeria (Isiugo-Abanihe, 1985), and Botswana (Frank, 1985). Regular sample surveys focused on the usual dimensions of demographics, such as fertility, mortality, nuptiality, and migration, as these are able to provide vital information on the practice of fosterage in this subregion of the African continent, from the perspective of the out-fostering parents and the foster families (Cissé, 1997; Fassassi, 1997; Pilon, 1995; Guillaume et al., 1994; Guillaume & Vimard, 1990; Quesnel & Vimard, 1988; Vimard & N'Cho, 1988; Vimard, 1987a, 1987b; Locoh, 1986; Antoine & Guillaume, 1986).

Studies in Ghana since the 1970s have demonstrated that, for working mothers, fostering out a young family member is a strategy for reconciling their reproductive role and their participation in building the labor force (Lloyd, 1970; Brydon, 1979; Date-Bah, 1986; Oppong & Abu, 1987; Isiugo-Abanihe, 1985). Available data from a recent study, which provide further support for this idea, demonstrate that mothers working at home are less likely to foster out their children through the age of five than mothers working outside the home (Blanc & Lloyd, 1990). Other studies have identified that the number of children in a given household has a direct correlation on fosterage. The higher the number of younger siblings, the more likely it is for a child to be fostered out (Lloyd & Desai, 1992). Studies have yet to be conducted on women's status in their households, the socioeconomic and demographic characteristics of household members, as well as the socioeconomic status of households regarding the role of economic motivations in the decision to out-foster.

In sub-Saharan Africa, it is more likely than not for a woman's social status to be dependent heavily on her reproductive success and a large progeny (Caldwell, 1978). High fecundity ensures the continuity of the group, and subfecundity in a woman is considered a more serious social defect than male sterility; the result is disparaging treatment from members of the community, with some of these women being accused of witchcraft (Erny, 1988).

In Senegal, for example, a woman within the Jola community, unable to bear children, "occupies a marginal position; she is excluded from religious ceremonies and from the mainstream women's associations, brought under strong suspicion, and ultimately rejected by her husband's kin" (Journet, 1991). Having a limited number of children, having too few children of a particular gender, or simply being unable to have any children is a very unhappy state for women in this subregion (Lallemand, 1980). Accepting foster children may be a way of compensating for this deficiency (Jonckers, 1997). Interestingly, quantitative studies, which have focused explicitly on the reasons for in-fostering by households, rarely mention sterility (Findley & Diallo, 1988; Renne, 1993; Guillaume & Vimard, 1990). The child's biological mother is either reported to have died, divorced, or to have conceived the child out of wedlock.

Available literature has shown that within the Mossi tribe of Burkina Faso, women who are likely to foster children generally are of menopausal age (Lallemand, 1976); among the Kotokoli of Togo, young boys are fostered to their grandfathers (Lallemand, 1980). In Ghana, children through the age of six are usually fostered to a grandparent (Fiawoo, 1978; Goody, 1982). Among the Ga, a third of the children surveyed were fostered to a grandparent (Azu, 1974). Within the Mende tribe of Sierra Leone, the child is fostered by the grandmother or, occasionally, one of his mother's sisters, an aunt (Isaac & Conrad, 1982). A young couple that is yet to have a child may well foster one because there is the popular notion among the rural folks that this form of parenting is likely to raise the chances of having their progeny, and quickly too (Jonckers, 1997, p. 195).

In some societies, it is acceptable to have a young bride joining her husband accompanied by a young girl from her family, who plays an auxiliary role in food processing and other household activities. This custom is prevalent among most ethnic groups in Ghana and the Baoulé of Côte d'Ivoire. Unlike the Ghanaian tribes, the Baoulé will have a baby girl promised to a young girl before puberty and it is often on these terms: They will say to the young girl, "Here is your child who will accompany you to your husband's home in future" (Etienne, 1979). Demographic studies across the subregion rarely draw attention to this motivation.

Women who are past the reproductive stage of their lives or are subfecund often represent female-headed households (Tichit, 1994) and are expected to foster children more frequently. For these women, it provides some social recognition, especially if they are considered a failure to meet their marital or maternal expectations (Pilon, Seidou Mama, & Tichit, 1996). Some studies based on small sample analysis have shown a positive correlation between fostering and enhanced social status, such as within the Mende tribe of Sierra Leone (Isaac & Conrad, 1982). The same has been observed for city dwellers in Côte d'Ivoire, among whom this practice helps maintain links with their place of origin (Etienne & Etienne, 1968). On the other hand, large-scale surveys have rarely studied this question, except for children aged six to fourteen in Côte d'Ivoire (Ainsworth, 1992). Finally, birth spacing in sub-Saharan Africa is linked to a large extent to postpartum amenorrhea, resulting from prolonged breastfeeding (van de Walle & van de Walle, 1988). Birth intervals of less than eighteen months have been recorded (Ronsmans, 1996), and these closely spaced births are a cause of mortality among the older children whose health is compromised as a result of the high frequency in procreation. A pregnant woman's milk is considered unclean and therefore, dangerous for the nursling (Akoto & Hill, 1988). For these different reasons, a mother who has closely spaced pregnancies is more likely to foster out her child as a way of weaning the child earlier and more easily; and, she is more likely to be encouraged to go that route (Bledsoe & Isiugo-Abanihe, 1989). This practice increases the probability of a new pregnancy without endangering the child's health from prolonged breastfeeding (Pennington & Harpending, 1993) as it is believed that the mother's breast milk is noxious to the infant.

Currently, it is common practice in Ghana to find girls in late childhood sent to live with other adult relatives who reside in urban locations and are relatively more financially sound than their rural counterparts. Unlike adoption, fostering by kin does not terminate parental rights and does not involve a legal process (Goody, 1973, p. 181). The institution of fostering provides mutual benefit to both parties, as seen among the Gonja tribe of northern Ghana. In this arrangement, the *kabita* as it is called in the Gonja dialect, meaning female foster child, will assist with regular household duties in exchange for her daily sustenance and an opportunity to procure the household items she will need on assuming the role of a wife and mother.

Breakdown of Kinship Fostering as a Cultural Influence

It is difficult to quantify how much kinship fostering has changed over the years in rural Ghanaian communities, but a greater section of the Ghanaian population agrees that there has been considerable erosion of this institution over the years (Goody, 1973). Currently, there is no literature available, but it became apparent from the narratives of the participants that the decline in kinship fostering has led to rural–urban flow among young girls, especially from the northern belt of the country. It is too early to suggest that the effect of fostering on this migratory pattern is regional. However, it was more likely for the participants from the Northern Region of the country to suggest the decline in fosterage as one of the factors underlying their presence on urban streets, compared to their southern counterparts, and was gender specific with more female than male participants making this kind of association. In fact, all eleven participants of the focus group of the migrants from the Northern Region of the country were in agreement that the decline in fosterage and at times the challenges children are likely to face while in fosterage play a major role in their decision to leave their rural homes for urban streets.

In fact the participants from the north suggested that their parents, especially mothers, had had better opportunities through fosterage and did not necessarily have to work on urban streets to acquire the household items for marriage. Zaratu shared her childhood experience, when she was fostered by her aunt, who lived in another village.:

> When I was a little girl, my father sent me off to live with my aunt, Jinche. That was shortly after she gave birth to her first baby and needed help on the household chores. I was about six years old when my father sent me to assist her. I was told my aunt Jinche would raise me in accordance with our traditions and customs and nurture me into a very good wife in future. I was supposed to learn how to run household chores such as food processing, dishwashing, and the art of babysitting. I was sad leaving my home, but my mother reassured me that my aunt would take very good care of me. I was also told that within the confines of our traditions, my aunt Jinche would be the one to purchase all the basic household items I need when I was ready to get married. One day I was allowed to go back home to visit my parents. I looked forward to it because I was going to be able to tell my mother all the hardships I faced at aunt Jinche's home. She would spank me almost on a regular basis when I made mistakes, and I sometimes had to go to bed without dinner. I worked so diligently and

> constantly, and you will not believe this, aunt Jinche would not believe it on occasions when I was ill. Instead, she would claim I was faking it and would spank me. And whenever I disclosed this to my mother, she would express her displeasure and communicate that to my father, who unlike my mother would immediately dismiss these claims. This would normally give rise to an altercation between my father and aunt Jinche on one side and my Mom on the other side. My aunt and my mother to this day are not on speaking terms. My mother indicated quite emphatically that I am better off living with her in the poverty of our home than be a slave to an abusive aunt. The final verdict: I am on the streets of Accra because I have to make money to be able to prepare adequately for my marriage in the near future anyway.

Other participants mentioned the inadequacies of the fosterage system. Sixteen-year-old Minatu alluded to the fact that fosterage has lost favor. Minatu spoke about the forms of abuse associated with the current system of fosterage versus the decades past. She revealed that fosterage is no longer as desired as it was in times past, and suggested that it is losing its appeal among rural children, and fast. Minatu had this to say:

> The reason fosterage is no longer appealing in recent times in my view is that most people take in their rural relatives and have them stay and serve them until they are ready to go away and marry. Most people see it as a system that affords foster families the opportunity to abuse the kids in fosterage. We hear of stories where foster children are spanked mercilessly and have gone without food sometimes. In some cases, foster families use these children for extended periods of time and ultimately send them back empty handed, quality time wasted. Some foster families also promise to provide these rewards at the beginning but later renege on their promises.

Instances of unsuccessful kinship fosterage were revealed through the narratives from some of the male participants in the cohort. Fifteen-year-old Moro, who migrated from northern Ghana and is one of six children in his family, indicated he was placed in fosterage because his parents could not afford to support them all. Asked where his siblings currently live, Moro responded, "One lives with my aunt, and the others, with my grandmother." Moro went further to indicate that he is here to work and raise money for school instead of living with his uncle because "I will just be home and will be unable to pursue my aspirations."

The narratives of these children are indicative of how much the system of fosterage has lost favor in recent times. Rural youth see no incentive in that direction and instead prefer to change course, perceiving the urban communities as more attractive hubs that will fulfill their dreams and aspirations, which seem to be fading away. For these children, it is always a race against time on treacherous terrain.

Mma Sharifa, a mother whom I met at Buipe, a northern fishing community located along the Black Volta River, shared her sentiments that corroborated claims by the northern girls. I spoke to her at the village market where she sells farm produce. Mma Sharifa lamented the fact that the Ghanaian economy is crumbling, and it is even more crushing for the rural folk. She went on to indicate that fostering thrived in the past when the economy flourished. She stated that there were rural families that had the financial capability in those times to foster their rural relatives. She talked about her own brother Baba Alhassan, who fostered in a number of children from within their family but had to let these children return to their biological parents, as his agricultural business was failing to yield the expected returns. He had no option but to make this difficult decision. She lamented the loss of this opportunity and attributed it to the out-migration they were experiencing in the village. She said:

> Fostering is part of our tradition. It was practiced by our ancestors and handed down to subsequent generations. Many generations have utilized and benefited from it. Within our family, my great grandmother, my grandmother, my mother, and myself were fostered. It was an avenue for learning our customs, and by the end

> of the period, one was well processed and ready for adulthood. Our foster parents were considered our parents too, and they are the ones who nurtured us. We grew up in very loving environments and enjoyed being with other relatives who were fostered too. Of course, those were the days before this economic downturn. I sit here all day and try to sell this stuff, but people can't come up with money and so we barely sell anything. A lot of people buy these items on credit and are unable to pay. I understand their situation since we are all in the same situation, and so I exercise much restraint. The few families who still practice fostering sometimes abuse the children because of the stress they have to endure as a result of the poverty that stares at them right in the face. Some of us went all the way to Kumasi and Accra to live with relatives. Presently, life in Accra is challenging because they are not willing any more to foster any of our kids from this village. Our ancestors will be very sad to know that this tradition is dying a slow death and will become history in the near future. Fostering reinforced the fact that we are all one family.

The phenomenon of rural–urban migration, a social pandemic as I choose to call it, is real and appears to be spreading at an alarming rate, knowing no boundaries. Are these children so inconspicuous that we do not see them around us? Are their voices so inaudible to attract the attention they so desperately need? Do these children have anything to offer their communities, regions, countries, and the world as a whole? Are they legitimate members of our community? Do they have any potential that can be harnessed to make our world a better place for our generation and those to come? From the preceding narratives, it appears justice and equity are fast becoming endangered aspects of the moral fabric of our society. We can and must present a sustainable, unified front against this ever-mounting equal-opportunity social ill that appears to be making giant strides and permeating every society on our planet each passing day. Together, we can establish better societies for future generations by affording today's human resource the opportunity to flourish, for we all live downstream.

Chapter Seven
Conclusion

Poverty, especially in many of the countries in the developing world, is at the root of most of the disadvantages street children face. The presence of children on urban streets is a "cross-country" problem. Discrimination appears to be the most troubling of the array of challenges these children on the streets face. What is disturbing is that the very urban contour, by law, is a designated "public" space. However, the presence of these young citizens in these areas is acutely perceived by authorities and other members of the society as illegitimate and totally unacceptable. Often, these children are rounded up in occasional substandard raids by law enforcement or clean-up squads and taken into custody or placed in some sort of confinement. It must be remembered that in most countries around the world, the urban landscape is usually dominated by individuals who wield economic and political power. Any intruders, such as outsiders like street children, are considered undesirable and face potential resentment, intimidation, abuse, and ultimately retribution by law enforcement and/or individuals who take the law into their own hands.

It is not surprising that street children have become the "rearguards," last to go to bed when the day comes to a close, and the harbingers or "vanguards" when the rooster crows. Whether they are built for this purpose or not, like wildebeests they are always on the move on this treacherous, unforgiving terrain. It is not surprising that many believe the most serious threat to street children comes from the very people responsible for their safety and protection—local governmental and law enforcement officials. While the lives of these young individuals may be romanticized by a small section of the public, they are often assigned derogatory labels around the world, some of which are *kuborlor* (runaway) in Ghana; *gamin* (urchin) and *chinches* (bed bugs) in Colombia; *marginais* (criminals/marginals) in Rio de Janeiro; *pajaro frutero* (fruit birds) in Peru; *polillas* (moths) in Bolivia; *resistoleros* (little rebels) in Honduras; *scugnizzi* (spinning tops) in Naples; *bui doi* (dust children) in Vietnam; *saligoman* (nasty kids) in Rwanda, or *poussins* (chicks); *moustiques* (mosquitos) in Cameroon; and *balados* (wanderers) in Zaire and Congo . . . and the list continues. It is perceived that these terms are adopted as justification for the discrimination and inhumane treatment to which these children are subjected, a clear indication of the density of the veil over our eyes.

Whether it is instinctive or learned behavior, what is empirical is that children get hungry, and if they fail to find food by legitimate or conventional means, they will steal it. Neglected by society and government, street children are deprived of education, proper nutrition, and medical care. They suffer and die from various, often easily treatable, diseases ranging from head lice and skin parasite infestation to pneumonia, tuberculosis, and a host of sexually transmitted diseases, including, yet not limited to, gonorrhea, syphilis, and AIDS.

The very essence of this volume, as I have mentioned before, is to accentuate the need to comprehend the very information these children seek to convey in their own language, which very often policy makers and the rest of the general public fail to decode, rather than do the narration and interpretation for them. The real danger lies in the outsider-centered approach by which we seek to undo this knot. A classic illustration was provided by Jill Swart (1990) to indicate the pivotal nature in listening carefully to and understanding the very vivid stories and explanations of these young individuals who have become illegitimate or second-class citizens in their own motherland.

Swart described two boys during her research among street children in Johannesburg, South Africa, both of whom repeatedly depicted graveyards in their drawings, as shown in Figure 8. From an outsider adultist psychological perspective, an addiction to the attitudes, ideas, beliefs, and actions of adults within every society, Swart indicates, will lead to the interpretation that these children were certainly depressed and even fixated on death by suicide or some other natural cause.

However, the children's explanations revealed to Swart a completely different scenario, several light-years from the adultist mental picture assigned to these drawings. The interpretation was flawed based on the fact that the same elucidation was assigned the drawings portrayed by these individuals. In fact the two boys had quite distinct motivations for their drawings. In one case, the drawings represented the boy's return to a traumatic moment, "the symbol of his state of unhappiness," when a quarrel with his brothers and sisters at his mother's grave-side ensued, which effectively led to his inevitable presence on the streets of Johannesburg. On the other hand, the second boy was depicting the burial place of his beloved grandmother, to which he returned as a happy memory and chose to express his feeling by the phrase, "Graves is good." He then added, "I think about my Granny. . . . She loved me" (Swart, 1990, p. 26).

Another illustration noted by Konjit Keftew (1996) during her interaction with street children in Addis Ababa, Ethiopia, as part of a pilot research project was with a twelve-year-old boy's conspicuous, lively self-portrait festooned in red and green colors. The boy depicted himself in this drawing wearing a hat, with a box of objects resting in front of him and one hand at his mouth. At first glance, it appeared the boy had depicted himself as one of the fruit vendors by the roadside of the community, with the hat apparently incidental. His explanation was completely different: The box contains rotten fruit, he said, and the hat component of the drawing is a way to conceal his face because he is ashamed to be seen by pedestrians and motorists eating such substandard and degrading food. (Example provided by Konjit Keftew, 1996, who carried out a study of street children in Addis Ababa as part of the Local Research Support Project sponsored by Radda

Barnen, Ethiopia). This anecdote is an object lesson in both attitudes to street children and the interpretation of information about them. It is a common assumption that children who live and work on the street either have no moral values and/or are antisocial, yet this boy's depiction makes a strong case for the thousands of children around the world that speak with a high degree of social sensitivity and dignity, but in a silent language (Ennew, 2003).

I do not know what tomorrow brings to the doorstep of these children and the rest of our global community, as these individuals continue their treacherous and intense march to the social and economic freedom that every child around the world deserves, and rightfully so. It must be emphasized that the "tomorrow" of these children certainly depends on what we provide them today. We must offer more than just sympathy, if these children are fortunate to receive this gesture. I am tempted to believe that not a single individual, but the local and global community, has the "Midas touch" to reverse this degrading downtrend.

For now, the question posed by Adjoa, "But where are the street children?" will linger on as long as we fail to change course or at least assign this phenomenon a realistic definition. If there is another world out there waiting to supplant ours, it is my cherished hope that it will be without the underclass of innocent individuals that currently inundates our community. Until then, our sorry reality lies in the fact that this phenomenon rages on relentlessly with immense and unstoppable momentum, knowing no boundaries.

Bibliography

Acheampong, O. 1996. *Tourism and Regional Development in Sub-Saharan Africa: A Case Study of Ghana's Central Region*. Stockholm: Stockholm University.

Ackah, C. and O. Morrissey. September 2005. "Trade Policy and Performance in Sub-Saharan Africa since the 1980s," Economic Research Working Paper No. 78, African Development Bank.

Adepoju, A. 1993. "Introduction," in A. Aderamto, ed., *The Impact of Structural Adjustment on the Population of Africa*. London: UNFPA/James Currey, pp. 1–24.

Adjibolosoo, S. and B. Afar-Amoah, eds. 1998. *Addressing Misconceptions about Africa's Development: Seeing Beyond the Veil*. Lewiston, NY: Edwin Mellen Press.

Aeroe, A. 1992. "Small Towns Development in Africa." *Geography Review* 6, 31–34.

African Forum and Network on Debt and Development. 2007. *Nigeria: Foreign Debts, Stolen Wealth, IFIs and the West. A Case Study*. AFRODAD.

Ainsworth M. 1992. "Economic Aspects of Child Fostering in Côte d'Ivoire, in Living Standards Measurement Study." Working Paper No. 92. Washington, DC: World Bank.

Akoto, E. and A. Hill. 1988. "Morbidité, Malnutrition et Mortalité des Enfants," in D. Tabutin, *Population et Sociétés en Afrique du Sud du Sahara*. Paris: L'Harmattan, pp. 309–334.

Aluworks Limited. http://www.aluworks.com. Retrieved April 13, 2010.

Amin, S. 1990. *Maldevelopment: Anatomy of a Global Failure*. London: Zed; Tokyo: United Nations University Press.

Anderson, K. and W. Martin. June 2006. *World Bank Economic Review* 20(2).

Anderson, M. and R. Rathbone. 2000. "Urban Africa: Histories in the Making," in D. Anderson and R. Rathbone, eds., *Africa's Urban Past*. Oxford: James Currey, pp. 1–17.

Andræ, G. 1981. *Industry in Ghana*. Uppsala: Scandinavian Institute of African Studies.

Antoine, P., M. Djire and J. Nanitelamio. 1998. "Au Coeur des Relations Hommes-Femmes: Polygamie et Divorce," in P. Antoine, D. Ouédragroa and V. Piché, eds., *Trois Générations de Citadins au Sahel*. Paris: L'Harmattan (Coll. Villes et entreprises), pp. 147–180.

Antoine, P. and A. Guillaume. 1986. "Une Expression de la Solidarité Familiale à Abidjan: Enfants du Couple et Enfants Confiés," in *Les Familles D'aujourd'hui, Aidelf*, No. 2. Paris: INED, pp. 17–29.

Apt Van Ham, N., E. Blave and S. K. Opoku. 1992. "Street Children in Accra: A Survey Report." Accra, University of Ghana Assibey-Mensah, G. O. 1998. Ghana's Women in Development Program. *Journal of Black Studies*, 29(2), 277–295.

Aryeetey, E., J. Harrigan and M. Nisanke, eds. 2000. *Economic Reforms in Ghana: The Miracle and the Mirage*. Oxford: James Currey and Woeli Publishers.

Ayee, J. 1997. "The Adjustment of Central Bodies to Decentralization: The Case of the Ghanaian Bureaucracy." *African Studies Review*, 40, 37–57.

Azani, R. 2005. "Profligacy, Corruption and Debt." *Daily Times*, Pakistan, February 10.

Azu D. 1974. "The Ga Family and Social Change." Leiden: African Social Research Documents, vol. 5. Cambridge: African Studies Centre.

Babatunde, M. A. 2009. "Can Trade Liberalization Stimulate Export Performance in Sub-Saharan Africa?" *Journal of International and Global Economic Studies*, 2(1), June, 68–92.

Baker, J., and P. Pedersen, eds. 1992. *The Rural-Urban Interface in Africa—Expansion and Adaptation*. Uppsala: Scandinavian Institute of African Studies.

Baran, P. 1957. "The Political Economy of Growth." *Monthly Review Press*, New York.

Barker, C., M. Bhagavan, P. Mitschke-Collande and D. Wield. 1986. *African Industrialization: Technology and Change in Tanzania*. Brookfield, VT: Gower.

Barker, K., P. Boateng and A. Moreno. 1991. "Timber and Wood Products Section of Export Diversification in Ghana." Report prepared for the US Agency for International Development. Bethesda, MD: Development Associates Inc.

Baron, S. and T. Hartnagel. 1998. "Street Youth and Criminal Violence." *Journal of Research in Crime and Delinquency*, 35(2), 166–188.

Beauchemin, E. 1999. "The Exodus: The Growing Migration of Children from Ghana's Rural Areas to Urban Centres." Catholic Action for Street Children and UNICEF. Ghana. Unpublished Manuscript. http://www.btinternet.com/~cas/exodus.htm. Retrieved April 15, 2002.

Bender-Pari, A. 1997. "On Their Own: Female Adolescents Who Run and the Reasons They Do." Masters thesis, Department of Social Work, California State University.

Bengston, V. and K. Allen. 1993. "The Life Course Perspective Applied to Families Over Time," in P.G. Boss, W. J. Doherty, R. LaRossa, W. R. Schumm and S. K. Steinmetz, eds., *Sourcebook of Family Theories and Methods: A Contextual Approach*. New York: Plenum, pp. 469–499.

Berg, B. 2001. *Qualitative Research Methods for the Social Sciences* (4th edition. Boston: Allyn and Bacon.

Berg, R. and J. Whitaker, eds. 1986. *Strategies for African Development*. Berkeley: University of California.

Biersteker, T., ed. 1993. *Dealing With Debt: International Financial Negotiations and Adjustment Bargaining*. Oxford: Westview Press.

Billsborrow R., T. McDevitt, S. Kassoudji and R. Fuller. 1987. "The Impact of Origin Community Characteristics on Rural-Urban Out-migration in a Developing Country." *Demography*, 24(2), 191–210.

Bird, G. 2001. "IMF Programs: Do They Work? Can They Be Made to Work Better?" *World Development*, vol. 29, no.11.

Blanc, A. and C. Lloyd. 1990. "Women's Childrearing Strategies in Relation to Fertility and Employment in Ghana." Working Paper No. 16. New York, NY: Population Council.

———. 1994. "Women's Work, Child-bearing and Child-rearing over the Life Cycle in Ghana," in A. Adepoju and C. Oppong, *Gender, Work and Population in Sub-Saharan Africa*. London: James Currey, pp. 112–131.

Bledsoe, C. 1989. "Differential Care of Children of Previous Unions Within Mende Households in Sierra Leone," in J. Caldwell et al., eds., *The Cultural, Social and Behavioural Determinants of Health*. Canberra: Health Transition Centre, Australian National University, pp. 561–583.

———. 1994. "The Social Construction of Reproductive Outcomes: Social Marginalization in Sub-saharan Africa," in T. Locoh and V. Hertrich, *The Onset of Fertility Transition in Sub-Saharan Africa*. Liège: IUSSP/Derouaux/ Ordina Editions, pp. 221–234.

Bledsoe C. and U. Isiugo-Abanihe. 1989. "Strategies of Child-fosterage among the Mende Grannies in Sierra Leone," in R. Lesthaeghe, *Reproduction and Social Organization in Sub-Saharan Africa*. Berkeley: University of California Press.

Blumer, H. 1969. *Symbolic Interactionism: Perspective and Method*. Englewood Cliffs, NJ: Prentice Hall.

Bocquier, P. 1996. "L'Analyse des Enquêtes Biographiques à L'Aide du Logiciel *STATA*." Paris: CEPED, Documents et Manuel du CEPED, No. 4.

Bop, C. 1996. "Les Femmes Chefs De Famille à Dakar," in J. Bisilliat, *Femmes du Sud, Chefs de Famille*. Paris: Khartala, pp. 129–149.

Boratav, K., O. Turel and E. Yeldan. 1996. "Dilemmas of Structural Adjustment and Environmental Policies Under Instability: Post-1980 Turkey." *World Development Report* 24. Washington, DC: World Bank, pp. 373–393.

Boss, P., W. Doherty, R. LaRossa, W. Schumm and S. Steinmetz, eds. *Sourcebook of Family Theories and Methods: A Contextual Approach*, New York: Plenum.

Briggs, J., Yeboah, I. 2001. "Structural Adjustment and the Contemporary sub-Saharan African City." *Area* 33, 18–26.

Bromley, S. 1995. "Making Sense of Structural Adjustment." *Review of African Political Economy*, 65, 339–348.

Brooks, J., A. Croppenstedt and E. Aggrey-Fynn. 2006. "Distortions to Agricultural Incentives in Ghana." Unpublished Manuscript. Rome: FAO.

Bryceson, D. 2001. "Countryside and City: Balancing or Blurring Differences?" in J. Schmidt and K. Gough, K., eds. *Urban Development in a Transitional Context*. Aalborg: Centre for Development and International Relations, Aalborg University pp. 192–219.

Brydon L. 1979. "Women at Work, Some Changes in Family Structure, Amedzofe-Avatime, Ghana," *Africa*, 49(2), 97–111.

Burchill, S. A. Linklater, R. Devetak and J. Donnelly. 1996. *Theories of International Relations*. London: Macmillan Press Limited.

Burrows, S. "The Role of Indigenous NGOs in the Development of Small Town Enterprises in Ghana," in J. Baker and P. Pedersen, eds. *The Rural-Urban Interface in Africa – Expansion and Adaptation*. Uppsala: Scandinavian Institute of African Studies, 1992, pp. 187–199.

Caldwell, J. 1968. "Determinants of Rural-Urban Migration in Ghana." *Population Studies*, 22(3), 361–377.

———. 1969. *African Rural-Urban Migration: The Movement to Ghana's Towns*. London: C. Hurst.

———. 1978. "Toward a Restatement of Demographic Transition Theory," *Population and Development Review*, 2(3–4), pp. 321–366.

Canagarajah, S. and D. Mazumdar. 1997. *Employment, Labour Markets and Poverty in Ghana: A Study of Changes during Economic Decline and Poverty*. Washington, DC: World Bank, 1997.

Cauce, A. M. and C. J. Morgan, 1994. "Effectiveness of Intensive Case Management for Homeless Adolescents: Results of a 3-Month Follow up." *Journal of Emotional and Behavioral Disorders*, 2(4), 219–227.

Central Bureau of Statistics (CBS). 1983. *Quarterly Digest of Statistics* (June). Accra, Ghana: CBS/Statistical Service Board.

Central Intelligence Agency. 2010. "The World Factbook–Ghana." US CIA. https://www.cia.gov/library/publications/the-world-factbook/geos/gh.html. Retrieved April 13, 2010.

Chang, H. and A. Singh. 1993. "Public Enterprises in Developing Countries and Economic Efficiency." *UNCTAD Review*, no. 4: 45–82

Charbit, Y. K. Ndiaye, S. Ndiaye, A. Sadio and I. Sarr. 1989. "Nuptialité et Fécondité au Sénégal," *Les Annales de l'Iford*, 13(2), 37–74.

Cherry, A. 1993. "Combining Cluster and Discriminant Analysis to Develop a Social Bond Typology of Runaway Youth." *Research on Social Work Practice* 3(2), 175–190.

Cheryl, P. 1974. *The Debt Trap: The IMF and Third World.* Middlesex, UK: Penguin Books Ltd.

Cisse, M. 1997. "Le 'Confiage' des Enfants à Dakar: Etude du Phénomène d'Accueil," dissertation Dess de démographie, supervised by J. Wakam. Université de Yaoundé II, Iford, République du Cameroun, 68.

CNN. 2009. "Obama's Ghana Trip Sends Message across Africa." http://wwwcnn.com/2009/WORLD/africa/07/10/ghana.obama/ index.html. Retrieved April 13, 2010.

Cody, J., H. Hughes and D. Wall, eds. *Policies for Industrial Progress in Developing Countries*. New York: Oxford University Press.

Collier, P. and J. Gunning. 1999. "Why Has Africa Grown Slowly?" *Journal of Economic Perspectives*, 13(3) Summer, 3–22.

Combé, J. 1972. *Forest Exploitation and Woodworking Industries in a Developing Country: Case Study of Ghana*. Memoire presented for the Diploma of the Institute, Geneva/FPRI, JUST, Kumasi, Ghana.

Cook, D. and J. Birchum. 1997. "Down on the Drag." *Texas Monthly*, January.

Crook, R. and J. Manor. 1998. *Democracy and Decentralization in South Asia and West Africa: Participation, Accountability and Performance*. Cambridge: Cambridge University Press.

CUS. 1990. "The Urban Poor in Dhaka," Dhaka, Bangladesh: *Centre for Urban Studies.*

Dare, S. 2001. "A Continent in Crisis, Africa and Globalization." *Dollars and Sense Magazine*, July/August.

Darkoh, M. 1971. "Industrial Location in a Developing Country: A Study of the Distribution of Manufacturing in Ghana in Relation to Selected Socioeconomic Characteristics." PhD diss. Madison: University of Wisconsin.

———. 1973. "Industrial Strategy and Rural Development in Africa with Special Reference to Ghana." *Geoforum*, 16, 7–24.

Date-Bah, E. 1986. "Sex Segregation and Discrimination in Accra-tema: Causes and Consequences," in R. Anker and C. Hein, *Sex Inequalities in Urban Employment in the Third World.* London: Macmillan Press, pp. 235–276.

Deaton, A. 1999. "Commodity Prices and Growth in Africa." *Journal of Economic Perspectives*, 13(3) Summer, 23–40.

de Soto, H. 1989. *The Other Path: The Invincible Revolution in the Third World.* New York: Harper and Row.

Dickson, K 1971. *A Historical Geography of Ghana.* Cambridge: Cambridge University Press.

———. 1975. "Development Planning and National Integration in Ghana," in D. Smock and K. Bentsi-Enchill, eds., *The Search for National Integration in Africa.* New York: Free Press, pp. 100–116.

Diversi, M. 1998. "Glimpses of Street Life: Representing Lived Experience Through Short Stories." *Qualitative Inquiry*, 4(2), 131–147.

Dupire, M. 1988. "L'ambiguïté Structurale du Fosterage Dans Une Société Matri-virilocale (Sereer Ndut, Sénégal)," *Anthropologie et Sociétés*, 12(2), 7–24.

The Economist. 1989. "A Change in Africa." September 3, p. 40.

———. 2002. "Band on the Run." July 4, pp. 32–33.

Ek, C. A. and L. C Steelman. 1988. "Becoming a Runaway from the Accounts of Youthful Runners." *Youth and Society*, 19(3), 334–358.

Eloundou-Enyegue, P. M. and C. S. Stokes. 2002. "Will Economic Crises in Africa Weaken Rural-Urban Ties? Insights from Child Fosterage Trends in Cameroon." *Rural Sociology* 67(2), 278–298.

Engberg-Pederson, P., P. Gibbon, P. Raikes and L. Udshot, eds. 1996. *Limits of Adjustment in Africa: The Effects of Economic Liberalization, 1986–94*. Portsmouth, NH: Heinemann.

Ennew, J. 2003. "Difficult Circumstances: Some Reflections on 'Street Children' in Africa." *Children, Youth and Environments* 13(1).

Epstein, I. 1996. "Educating Street Children: Some Cross-Cultural Perspectives." *Comparative Education* 32(3), 289–302.

Erny, P. 1988. *Les Premiers Pas dans La Vie de L'enfant*. Paris: L'Harmattan.

Etienne, M. 1979. "Maternité Sociale, Rapports D'adoption et Pouvoir Des Femmes Chez Les Baoulé (Côte D'ivoire)." *L'homme*, 19(3–4), 63–107.

Etienne, P. and M. Etienne. 1968. "L'émigration Baoulé actuelle," *Les cahiers d'Outre-Mer*, 82, 155–195.

Extreme Points of Earth. http://en.wikipedia.org/wiki/Extreme_points_of_Earth. Retrieved April 13, 2010.

Ewusi, K. 1987. *Structural Adjustment and Stabilization Policies in Developing Countries: A Case Study of Ghana's Experience in 1983–1986*. Legon, Ghana: ISSER, University of Ghana.

Fentimen, A. and A. Hall. 1999. "School Enrolment Patterns in Rural Ghana: A Comparative Study of the Impact of Location, Gender, Age and Health on Children's Access to Basic Schooling." *Comparative Education*, 35(3), 331–349.

Fiawoo, D. 1978. "Some Patterns of Foster Care in Ghana," in C. Oppong et al., *Marriage, Fertility and Parenthood in West Africa*. Canberra: Australian National University, 273–288.

Fik, T. 1999. *The Geography of Economic Development: Regional Changes, Global Challenges*. 2nd ed. New York: McGraw Hill.

Findley, S. and A. Diallo. 1988. "Foster Children: Links Between Urban and Rural Families," in *African Population Conference*, vol. 2. Dakar: IUSSP, 43–57.

Finger, J. and P. Schuler. 2001. "'Implementation of Uruguay Round Commitments: The Development Challenge', Ch. 7," in B. Hoekman and W. Martin, eds., *Developing Countries and the WTO: A Pro-Active Agenda*. Oxford: Blackwell.

Finger, J. and L. Winters. 2002. "'Reciprocity in the WTO', Ch. 7," in B. Hoekman, A. Matoo, and P. English, eds. *Development, Trade and the WTO: A Handbook*. Washington, DC: World Bank.

Finley, S. 1999. "SP'ANGE: A Research Story." *Qualitative Inquiry*, 5(3), 313–337.

Fischer, B. 1990. "Developing Countries in the Process of Economic Globalization." *Intereconomics*, March/April, 55–63.

Fopp, R. 1993. "More Heat than Houses." *Youth Studies*, 12(2), 45–50.

Frank, A. 1971. *Crisis in The Third World*. London: Heinemann.

Frank, O. 1985. "La Mobilité des Enfants et L'autosuffisance Économique Des Femmes Dans Le Milieu Patriarcal Africain," in J. Bisilliat et al., *Femmes et Politiques Alimentaires*. Paris, ORSTOM-CIE, pp. 641–652.

Ghana Poverty Reduction Strategy (GPRS). 2002. Accra: Ministry of Finance/ Government of Ghana, February.

Giddens, A. 1991. *The Consequences of Modernity*. Stanford, CA: Stanford University Press.

Glesne, C. and P. Alan. 1992. *Becoming Qualitative Researchers: An Introduction*. White Plains, NY: Longman.

Global Network on Local Governance, Institute of Social Sciences (ISS). 2008. http://www.gnlg.org/global-network-local-governance1.asp?sub_ id=135&sub_ menu=DECENTRALISATION&id=9.

Goody, E. 1972. "Conjugal Separation and Divorce among the Gonja of Northern Ghana," in Meyer Fortes, ed., *Marriage in Tribal Societies: Cambridge Papers in Social Anthropology*. Cambridge: Cambridge University Press.

———. 1973. *Contexts of Kinship: An Essay in the Family Sociology of the Gonja of Northern Ghana*. Cambridge: Cambridge University Press.

———. 1982. *Parenthood and Social Reproduction: Fostering and Occupational Roles in West Africa*. Cambridge: Cambridge University Press.

Grant, R. Yankson, P. 2003. "Accra." *Cities*, 20, 65–74.

Green, A. and R Leech, eds. 2003. *Cities in the World*. London: SPMA/Maney Publications.

Green, R. 1987. *Stabilization and Adjustment Policies and Programmes. Country Study 1: Ghana*. Annankatu, Finland: World Institute for Development and Economic Research.

———. 1991. *Reduction of Absolute Poverty: A Priority Structural Adjustment*. Discussion paper 287. Sussex: Institute of Development Studies.

Greenberg, J. 1997. "A Political Ecology of Structural-Adjustment Policies: The Case of the Dominican Republic." *Culture & Agriculture*, 19(3), 85–93.

Greene, J., S. Ennett and C. Ringwalt. 1997. "Substance Use among Runaway and Homeless Youth in Three National Samples." *American Journal of Public Health*, 87(2), 299–305.

GSS (Ghana Statistical Service). 2000. *Poverty Trends in Ghana in the 1990s*. Accra: GSS.

———. 1995. *Migration Research Study in Ghana*, vol. 1, *Internal Migration*. Accra: GSS.

———. 2002a. *Population and Housing Census—Summary Report of Final Result*. Accra: GSS.

Guillaume, A. and P. Vimard. 1990. *Santé de la Mère et de L'enfant et Dynamique Familiale à Sassandra*. Paris: Études et Recherches ENSAE, ORSTOM, UNICEF.

Guillaume, A., P. Vimard, R. Fassassi, and K. N'guessan. 1994. "La Circulation des Enfants en Côte-d'ivoire: Solidarité Familiale et Redistribution De Main-d'oeuvre," in *Colloque International Crise, Ajustements et Recompositions en Côte D'ivoire: La Remise en Cause d'un Modèle*, séance No. 5, 28 Nov.–2 Dec.. Abidjan, ORSTOM-GIDIS-CI, pp. 11–22.

Hamilton, C. 1989. "The Irrelevance of Economic Liberalization in the Third World." *World Development* 17 (10). Washington, D.C.: World Bank, 1523–30.

Hawkins, A. 1986. "Can Africa Industrialize?" in R. Berg and J. Whitaker, eds., *Strategies for African Development*. Berkeley: University of California, pp. 279–307.

Heir, S. and P. Korboot. 1999. "Social Adjustment and Symptomatology in Two Types of Homeless Adolescents: Runaways and Throwaways." *Adolescence*, 25(100), 761–769.

Helleiner, G. 1995. *Trade, Trade Policy, and Industrialization Reconsidered.* Helsinki: World Institute for Development Economics Research.

Hoekman, B., A. Matoo and P. English, eds. 2002. *Development, Trade and the WTO: A Handbook.* Washington, DC: World Bank.

Hoekman, M. (ed.) 2001. *Developing Countries and the WTO: A Pro-Active Agenda.* Oxford: Blackwell.

Holsti, K. 1995. *International Politics: A Framework for Analysis.* Princeton, NJ: Princeton International Inc.

Hughes, H. 1980. "Achievements and Objectives of Industrialization." in J. Cody, H. Hughes, and D. Wall, eds., *Policies for Industrial Progress in Developing Countries.* New York: Oxford University Press, pp. 11–37.

Huq, M. 1989. *The Economy of Ghana.* London: Macmillan Press.

Hyden, G., H. Okoth-Ogendo and B. Olowu, eds. 2000. *African Perspective on Governance.* Trenton, NJ: Africa World Press.

Ikejiaku, B. 2008. "The Relationship Between Poverty, Peace and Development in Africa, Political Corruption Emphasized 1960–2007: Case Studies of Nigeria and South Africa," Unpublished PhD Thesis, Keele University, UK: School of Politics, International Relations and Philosophy.

———. 2009. "The Relationship between Poverty, Conflict and Development." *Journal of Sustainable Development*, 2(1) March.

"International Religious Freedom Report, 2007." U.S. Department of State. http://www.state.gov/g/drl/rls/irf/2007/90100.htm. Retrieved April 13, 2010.

Isaac, B. and S. Conrad. 1982. "Child Fosterage among the Mende of Upper Bambara Chiefdom, Sierra Leone: Rural-Urban and Occupational Comparisons." *Ethnology*, 21(3), 243–257.

Isiugo-Abanihe, U. 1985. "Child Fosterage in West Africa." *Population and Development Review*, 11(1), 53–73.

———. 1994. "Parenthood in Sub-Saharan Africa: Child Fostering and its Relationship with Fertility," in T. Locoh and V. Hertrich, eds., *The Onset of Fertility Transition in Sub-Saharan Africa*. Liège: IUSSP/Derouaux/Ordina Editions, pp. 163–174.

Jahangir, A. 2002. "Civil and Political Rights, Including the Question of Disappearances and Summary Executions." Special Report submitted at Fifty-ninth session of United Nations Commission on Human Rights Meeting on June 14, 2002.

Jonckers, D. 1997. "Les Enfants Confiés," in M. Pilon, T. Locoh, E. Vignikin and P. Vimard, eds., *Ménages et Familles en Afrique*. Paris: CEPED (Les Études du CEPED, No. 15), pp. 193–208.

Journet, O., 1991. "Un Rituel de Préservation de la Descendançe: Le Kanyaalen Joola," in S. Lallemand, O. Journet, E. Ewombé-Moundo, B. Ravololomanga, A. Dupuis, M. Cros and D. Jonckers, D., eds., *Grossesse et Petite Enfance en Afrique Noire et à Madagascar*. Paris: L'Harmattan (Coll. Connaissance des Hommes), pp. 19–40.

Kadioglu, A. 1994. "The Impact of Migration on Gender Roles: Findings from Field Research in Turkey." *International Migration*, 32(4), 533–561.

Khinduka, S. 1971. "Social Work in the Third World," *Social Service Review*, 45.

Konadu-Agyemang, K. 2000. "The Best Times and the Worst Times: Structural Adjustment Programs and Uneven Development in Africa." *Professional Geographer*, 52, 469–483.

———. 2001. *The Political Economy of Housing and Urban Development in Africa: Ghana's Experience from Colonial Times to 1998*. London: Praeger.

Konadu-Agyemang, K. and S. Adanu. 2003. "The Changing Geography of Export Trade in Ghana under Structural Adjustment Programs: Some Socioeconomic and Spatial Implications." *Professional Geographer*, 55, 513–527.

Kraev, E. 2004. "Structural Adjustment Policies in Ghana in the 1990s." An Empirical Analysis and Policy Recommendations UNDP Discussion Paper, School of Public Policy, University of Maryland, College Park.

———. 2004b. "Towards Adequate Analysis and Modeling of Structural Adjustment Programs: An Analytical Framework with Application to Ghana." PhD thesis, School of Public Policy, University of Maryland, College Park.

Krueger, A. 1992. "Global Trade Prospects for the Developing Countries." *The World Economy*, 15, 457–474.

Kryder-Coe, J., L. Salamon and J. Molnar. 1991. *Homeless Children and Youth: A New American Dilemma*. New Brunswick, NJ: Transaction Publishers.

Kurtz, D., S. Jarvis and G. Kurtz. 1991. "Problems of Homeless Youths: Empirical Findings and Human Services Issues." *Social Work*, 36(4), 309–313.

Lancy, D. 1993. *Qualitative Research in Education*. White Plains, NY: Longman.

Lallemand, S. 1976. "Génitrices et Éducatrices Mossi." *L'Homme*, 16(1), 109–124.

———. 1980. "L'adoption des Enfants Chez les Kotokoli du Togo." *Anthropologie et Sociétés*, 4(2), 19–37.

———. 1993. *La Circulation des Enfants en Société Traditionnelle, Prêt, don, Echange*. Paris: L'Harmattan (Coll. Connaissance des hommes).

———. 1994. *Adoption et Mariage, les Kotokoli du Centre du Togo*. Paris, L'Harmattan (Coll. Connaissance des hommes).

Lallemand, S., O. Journet, E. Ewombé-Moundo, B. Ravololomanga, A. Dupuis, M. Cros and D. Jonckers, eds. 1996. *Grossesse et Petite Enfance en Afrique Noire et À Madagascar*. Paris: L'Harmattan (Coll. Connaissance des Hommes).

Levine Powers, J. L., 1990. "Survivors of Abuse Tell Their Stories." *Human Ecology*, 18(2), 8–11.

Lewis, R. A., R. J. Volk and S. Duncan, 1989. "Stresses on Fathers and Family Relationships Related to Rural Youth Leaving and Returning Home.' *Family Relations*, 38, 174–81.

Little, K. 1957. "The Role of Voluntary Associations in West African Urbanization." *American Anthropologist, New Series*, 59(4), 579–596.

———. 1966. "Some Social Consequences." *African Affairs*, 65(259), 160–169.

———. 1974. *Urbanization as a Social Process*. London: Routledge.

Lloyd, B., 1970. "Yoruba Mothers' Reports of Child-rearing," in P. Mayer, *Socialization: The Approach from Social Anthropology*. London: Tavistock Publications, pp. 75–107.

Lloyd, C. and A. Blanc. 1996. "Children's Schooling in Sub-Saharan Africa: The Role of Fathers, Mothers, and Others." *Population and Development Review*, 22(2), 265–298.

Lloyd, C. and S. Desai. 1992. "Children's Living Arrangements in Developing Countries." *Research and Policy Review*, 11(3), 193–216.

Lloyd, C. and A. Gage-Brandon. 1993. "High Fertility and the Intergenerational Transmission of Gender Inequality; Children's Transition to Adulthood in Ghana," in Séminaire *Les Femmeset les Changements Démographiques en Afrique Au Sud du Sahara*, OrstOM. Dakar, Sénégal: IUSSP.

Lundy, K. 1993. "On the Edge: A Naturalistic Study of a Small Group of Street Kids." PhD dissertation, School of Education, Health, Nursing, and Arts Professions, New York University.

Mabogunje, A. 1981. *The Development Process: A Spatial Perspective*. New York: Holmes and Meier.

Mahoub, A., ed. *Adjustment or Delinking?: The African Experience.* Tokyo: United Nations University Press, pp. 131–156.

Meagher, K. 1995. "Crisis, Informalization, and the Urban Informal Sector in Sub-Saharan Africa." *Development and Change*, 23, 259–284.

Melson, B. 1995. "Runaway Adolescents: A Family Systems Perspective." New York: Garland Publishing.

Midgley, J. 1981. *Professional Imperialism: Social Work in the Third World.* London: Heinemann.

———. 1990. "International Social Work: Learning from the Third World." *Social Work*, (35)4, July.

Migdal, J. 1988. *Strong Societies and Weak States.* Princeton, NJ: Princeton University Press.

Moser, C. 1978. "Informal Sector Petty Commodity Production: Dualism or Dependence in Urban Development." *World Development* 6 (9/10). Washington, D.C.: World Bank, 1041–64.

Mufume, P. 2000. "Street Youth in Southern Africa." *International Social Science Journal*, 52(164), 233–243.

Mupedziswa, R. 1992. "Africa at the Crossroads: Major Challenges for Social Work Education and Practice towards the Year 2000." *Journal of Social Development in Africa*, 7(2).

Mytelka, L. 1989. "The Unfulfilled Promise of African Industrialization." *African Studies Review*, 32(3), 77–137.

Nabi, A. 1992. "Dynamics of Internal Migration in Bangladesh," *Canadian Studies in Population*, 19(1), 81–98.

Ninsin, K. 1990. "Ghana under the PNDC: Delinking or Structural Adjustment?" in A. Mahoub, ed., *Adjustment or Delinking?: The African Experience.* Tokyo: United Nations University Press, pp. 131–156.

Ninsin, K. 1991. *The Informal Sector in Ghana's Political Economy.* Accra, Ghana: Freedom Publications.

Nyanteng, V. and A. Seini. 2000. "Agricultural Policy and the Impact on Growth and Productivity 1970–95," in E. Aryeetey, J. Harrigan and M. Nissanke, eds., *Economic Reforms in Ghana, The Miracle and The Mirage*. Oxford: James Currey and Woeli Publishers.

Ofei-Nkansah, K. 1991. "Ghana's Timber Boom." *West Africa*, 3833 (February 18–24), 229.

Offiong, D. 1980a. *Imperialism and Dependence: Obstacles to African Development*. Enugu, Nigeria: Fourth Dimension.

———. 1989. *Imperialism and Dependency, Obstacles to African Development*. Enugu, Nigeria: Fourth Dimension Publishing Co.

Afar, S. 2002. *Regional Policy and Regional Planning in Ghana: Making Things Happen in the Territorial Community*. Aldershot: Ashgate.

Onimode, B. (ed.) 1989. *The IMF, the World Bank and the African Debt, The Economic Impact*. London: Zed Books.

Oppong, C. and K. Abu. 1987. *Seven Roles of Women: Impact of Education, Migration and Employment on Ghanaian Mothers*. Geneva: ILO.

Oppong, C. et al., eds. 1978. *Marriage, Fertility and Parenthood in West Africa*. Canberra: Australian National University.

Osei-Hwedie K., L. Mwansa, P. Mufune and G. Maipose, eds. *Towards Structural Adjustment in Zambia: An Overview*. Geneva: United Nations Research Institute for Social Development.

———. *Crisis, Adjustment and Social Change in Zambia. The Case of the Youth*. Geneva: United Nations Research Institute for Social Development.

———. 1990. "Social Work and the Question of Social Development in Africa." *Journal of Social Development in Africa*, 15(2).

Ould-Mey, M. 1996. *Global Restructuring and Peripheral States: The Carrot and the Stick in Mauritania*. Lanham, MD: Rowman & Littlefield.

Owusu, G. 2002. "Whose Space and Place? Ethical Implications of the 'Rural-Urban' Divide and Current Development Processes in Sub-Saharan Africa." *Acta Geographica Series* A, 220–226.

———. 2004. "Small Towns and Decentralised Development in Ghana: Theory and Practice." *Afrika Spectrum*, 39, 165–195.

———. 2005a. "The Changing Views on the Role of Small Towns in Rural and Regional Development in Sub-Saharan Africa," in A. Green and R. Leech, eds., *Cities in the World*. London: SPMA/Maney Publications.

———. 2005b. "The Role of District Capitals in Regional Development: Linking Small Towns, Rural-Urban Linkages and Decentralisation in Ghana." *International Development Planning Review*, 27.

Owusu, J. 1995. "Structural Adjustment and African Development: Evidence from Ghana's Formal Wood Processing Industry 1983–1991." *Review of Human Factor Studies*, 1(2), 60–79.

———. 1998a. "The Myth of Development under Ghana's Structural Adjustment Program: Evidence from the Formal Wood-processing Sector (1983–1991)," in S. Adjibolosoo and B. Afar-amoah, eds., *Addressing Misconceptions about Africa's Development: Seeing Beyond the Veil*. Lewiston, NY: Edwin Mellen Press, pp. 193–216.

———. 1998b. "Current Convenience, Desperate Deforestation: Ghana's Adjustment Program and the Forestry Sector." *Professional Geographer*, 50(4), 418–436.

———. 2001. "Spatial Integration, Adjustment, and Structural Transformation in Sub-Saharan Africa: Some Linkage Pattern Changes in Ghana." *Professional Geographer*, 53, 230–247.

Patterson-Taylor, E. 2000. "Homeless and Runaway Adolescents: A Study and Analysis." MSW thesis, Department of Social Work, California State University.

Peil, M. "Aspirations and Social Structure: A West African Example." *Africa: Journal of the International African Institute,* 38(1), 71–78.

Pennington, R. and H. Harpending. 1993. "Child Fosterage and Social Parenthood," in R. Pennington and H. Harpending, *The Structure of an African Pastoralist Community, Demography, History and Ecology of the Ngamiland Herero*. Oxford: Clarendon Press, pp. 171–199.

———. 1993. *The Structure of an African Pastoralist Community, Demography, History and Ecology of the Ngamiland Herero*. Oxford: Clarendon Press.

Pilon, M. 1995. "Les Déterminants de la Scolarisation des Enfants de 6–14 Ans au Togo en 1981: Apports et Limites Des Données Censitaires." *Cahiers des Sciences Humaines*, ORSTOM, 31(3), 697–718.

Pilon, M., T. Locoh, E. Vignikin and P. Vimard, eds. *Ménages et Familles en Afrique*, Paris: CEPED (Les Études du CEPED, No. 15).

Pilon, M., M. Seidou Mama and C. Tichit. 1996. "Les Femmes Chefs De Ménage: Aperçu Général et Études De Cas," in M. Pilon, T. Locoh, E. Vignikin and P. Vimard, eds., *Ménages et familles en Afrique*. Paris: CEPED (Les Études du CEPED, No. 15), pp. 167–191.

Pilon, M. and K. Vignikin. 1996. "Stratégies Face à la Crise et Changements dans les Structures Familiales," in J. Coussy and J. Vallin, eds., *Crise et Population en Afrique* (Les Études du CEPED, No 13). Paris: CEPED, pp. 471–493.

Potter, R., T. Binns, J. Elliott and D. Smith. 1999. *Geographies of Development*. London: Longman.

Powers, J. L. and B. Jacklitsch. 1993. "Reaching the Hard to Reach." *Education and Urban Society*, 25(4), 394–409.

Quesnel, A. and P. Vimard. 1988. "Dynamique de Population en Économie de Plantation, le Plateau de Dayes au Sud-ouest du Togo." Paris: Éditions de l'ORSTOM (Coll. Études et Thèses).

Quist, H. O. 2001. "Cultural Issues in Secondary Education in West Africa: Away From Colonial Survivals, Toward Neocolonial Influences?" *Comparative Education*, 37(3), 297–314.

Raffaelli, M., S. H. Koller, C. T. Reppold, M. B. Kuschick, F. M. B. Krum and D. R. Bandeira. 2001. "How do Brazillian Street Youth Experience "The Street"? Analysis of a Sentence Completion Task." *Childhood*, 8(3), 396–415.

Razin, E. and N. Obirih-Opareh. 2000. "Spatial Variations in the Fiscal Capacity of Local Government in Ghana, Before and After Decentralization." *Third World Planning Review*, 22, 411–432.

Renne, E. 1993. "History in the Making. An Anthropological Approach to the Demographic Analysis of Child Fostering in Southwestern Nigeria," in *International Population Conference*, Montreal: IUSSP, pp. 327–342.

Rigzone. 2008. "Kosmos Makes Second Oil Discovery Offshore Ghana." http://www.rigzone.com/news/article.asp?a_id=57319. Retrieved April 13, 2010.

Rodney, W. 1972. *How Europe Underdeveloped Africa*. London: Bogle L'Ouverture.

Roemer, M. 1981. "Dependence and Industrialization Strategies." *World Development*, 9(5), 429–434.

Ronsmans, C. 1996. "Birth Spacing and Child Survival in Rural Senegal," *International Journal of Epidemiology*, 25(5), 989–997.

Rosenblatt, P. and L. Fishcher. 1993. "Qualitative Family Research," in P. Boss, W. Doherty, R. LaRossa, W. Schumm and S. Steinmetz, eds., *Sourcebook of Family Theories and Methods: A Contextual Approach*, New York: Plenum, 167–177.

Rostow, W. 1960. *The Stages of Economic Growth*. Cambridge: Cambridge University Press.

Sachs, J. 2005. *The End of Poverty: How We Can Make it Happen in Our Life*. New York: Penguin.

Sandbrook, R. 1982. *The Politics of Basic Needs*. London: Heinemann.

Savane, L. 1994. "Le Confiage des Enfants à Pikine," in Y. Charbit and S. Ndiaye. "*La population du Sénégal*, Paris: DPS-CERPAA, 127–42.

Savané, M., ed. 1986. *Femmes et développement en Afrique de l'Ouest*, Geneva: UNRISD.

Savané, M. and K. Lyniango. 1986. "Incidences de la Modernisation de l'Agriculture sur le Role et le Statut des Femmes au Sénégal," in M. Savané, ed., *Femmes et Développement en Afrique de l'Ouest*. Geneva: UNRISD, 129–207.

Sawyerr, A. 1990. *The Political Dimension of Structural Adjustment Programmes in Sub-Saharan Africa*. Accra: Ghana Universities Press.

Sayer, Andrew. 1986. "New Developments in Manufacturing: The Just-in-time System." *Capital and Class*, 30, 43–72.

Schweitzer, R. and S. Heir. 1994 "Parental Bonding, Family Systems, and Environmental Predictors of Adolescent Homelessness." *Journal of Emotional and Behavioral Disorders*, 2(1), 39–45.

Sekhar, T. 1993. "Migration Selectivity from Rural Areas: Evidence from Kerala." *Demography India*, 22(2), 191–202.

Sender, J. 1999. "Africa's Economic Performance: Limitations of the Current Consensus." *Journal of Economic Perspectives*, 13(3), 89–114.

Shaffner, L. 1999. "Teenage Runaways: Broken Hearts and Bad Attitudes." New York: Hatworth Press.

Shanahan, P. 2002. "Street Child Africa: The Problem." http://www.streetchildafrica.org.uk. Retrieved October 29, 2002.

———. 2003. "Streets versus Elites: Tensions, Trade-offs, and Treaties with Street Children in Accra, Ghana." *Children, Youth and Environments*, 13(1), 1–9.

Shane, P. 1996. "What About America's Homeless Children? Hide and Seek." Sage Sourcebooks for the Human Services. Thousand Oaks, CA: SAGE Publications.

Simpson, E. 1994. *The Developing World: An Introduction*. 2nd ed. New York: Longman/Wiley and Sons.

Smith, B. 2003. *Understanding Third World Politics: Theories of Political Change and Development*. New York: Palgrave Macmillan.

Smock, D. and K. Bentsi-Enchill, eds. 1975. *The Search for National Integration in Africa*. New York: Free Press.

Songsore, J. and A. Denkabe. 1995. *Challenging Rural Poverty in Northern Ghana: The Case of the Upper West Region*. Trondheim: SMU, University of Trondheim.

Sowa, N. 1993. "Ghana," in A. Adepoju, ed., *The Impact of Structural Adjustment on the Population of Africa*. London: UNFPA, 1993, pp. 7–24.

Statistical Service. 1995. *Quarterly Digest of Statistics*, vol. 13, no. 1 (March). Accra: Government of Ghana.

———. 1997. *Quarterly Digest of Statistics*, vol. 15, no. 2 (June). Accra: Government of Ghana.

Steel, W. 1988. "Recent Policy Reform and Industrial Adjustment in Zambia and Ghana." *Journal of Modern African Studies*, 26, 157–164.

Storh, W. and D. Taylor, eds. 1981. *Development from Above or Below, The Dialectics of Regional Planning in Developing Countries*. Chichester, UK: John Wiley and Sons.

Swart, J. 1990. *Malunde: The Street Children of Hillbrow*. Johannesburg: Witwatersrand University Press.

Symons, Y. and R. Smith. 1995. "Noticed But Not Understood." *Youth Studies*, 14(1), 29–36.

Szerezewski, R. 1966. "The Sectoral Structure of the Economy of Ghana, 1960," in W. Birmingham, ed., *A Study of Contemporary Ghana*. London: Allen and Unwin, pp. 62–88.

Taback R. 1991. "The Movement Towards Indigenization of Social Service Delivery in South America." *Maatskaplike Werkl Social Work*, V0127, No. 3/4.

Taylor, L. 1988. *Varieties of Stabilization Experience – Towards Sensible Macro-economics of the Third World*. Oxford: Clarendon Press.

Teare, J. and R. Peterson. 1994. "Treatment Implementation in a Short-Term Emergency Shelter Program." *Child Welfare*, 73(3), 271–281.

Terrel, N. 1997. "Street Life Aggravated and Sexual Assaults among Homeless and Runaway Adolescents." *Youth and Society*, 28(3), 267–290.

Thomi, W. and P. Yankson. 1985. *Small Scale Industries and Decentralization in Ghana*. Accra: University of Ghana/J. W. Goethe Universitat.

Thompson, S., A. Safyer and E. Pollio. 2001. "Differences and Predictors of Family Reunification among Subgroups of Runaway Youths Using Shelter Services." *Social Work Research*, 25(3), 163–172.

Tichit, C. 1994. "La montée des Femmes Chefs de Ménage en Afrique du sud du Sahara: Examen à Partir des Données Publiées sur les Ménages," dissertation DEA, Paris: EHESS.

Timber Exports Development Board (TEDB). n.d. *The Ghana Timber Industry: Basic Information, Facts, and Figures*. Mimeo. Takoradi, Ghana: TEDB.

Tyler, K., D. Hoyt and L. Whitbeck. 2000. "The Effects of Early Sexual Victimization on Later Sexual Victimization among Female Homeless and Runaway Adolescents." *Journal of Interpersonal Violence*, 15(3), 235–250.

Unger, J., M. Kipke, et al. 1998. "Stress, Coping, and Social Support among Homeless Youth." *Journal of Adolescent Research*, 13(2), 134–157.

United Nations. 1987. *UN Centre for Social Development and Humanitarian Affairs: Social Development Newsletter, Special Issue, Inter-Regional Consultation on Developmental Social Welfare Policies and Programmes*, Part II Volume 1987–2, No 26.

———. 2007. *Human Development Report* (HDR), 2007. United Nations Development Program, November 27, 2007. New York: United Nations, p. 25.

———. 2010. *Human Development Indices*, "Table 3: Human and Income Poverty," p. 35. Retrieved April 13, 2010.

———. 2007. *The Millennium Development Goals (MDG) Report 2007*. United Nations. New York.

United Nations Economic Commission for Africa (UN/ECA). 1986. *African Alternative Framework to Structural Adjustment Programmes for Socioeconomic Recovery and Transformation (AAF-SAP)*. E/ECA/CM. 15/6/Rev. 3. New York: UN/ECA.

United Nations Economic and Social Council. 2008. *Achieving Sustainable Development and Promoting Development Cooperation: Dialogues at the Economic and Social Council*. New York: United Nations, Dept. of Economic and Social Affairs, Office for ECOSOC Support and Coordination.

Vandermeersch, C. 2000. "Les enfants confiés au Sénégal," Ph.D. thesis, Institut d'Études Politiques de Paris, Démographie économique.

Van de Walle, E. and F. Van de Walle. 1988. "Les Pratiques Traditionnelles et Modernes des Couples en Matière d'Espacement ou d'Arrêt de la Fécondité," in D. Tabutin, *Population et Sociétés en Afrique du Sud du Sahara*, Paris: L'Harmattan, pp. 141–165.

Van Dinther, J. 2000. "Catholic Action for Street Children: The Street Children." http://www.btinternet.com/~cas/st-child.htm. Retrieved October 29, 2002.

Vimard, P. 1987a. "Structure des Ménages en Pays Akye, Composition et Typologies Familiales à Memmi et Montezo," Abidjan: ORSTOM.

——— 1987b. "Structures des Ménages en Pays Baoulé. Composition et Typologies Familiales à Brobo (département de Baouké)," ENSEA-ORSTOM (Études et Recherches, No. 14).

Vimard, P. and S. N'cho. 1988. "Les Noyaux Familiaux en Côte d'Ivoire : Structures et Probabilities de Transition," in *African Population Conference*, vol. 2. Dakar: IUSSP, pp. 59–74.

Wakam, J. 1999. "Urbanisation et Structures Familiales des Ménages en Afrique. Aperçu General et cas Spécifiques du Cameroun, de la Côte d'Ivoire et du Sénégal," paper presented at the Chaire Quetelet *Populations et défis urbains*, Louvain-La-Neuve, October 26–29, 1999.

Wanyande, P. 1997. "State Driven Conflict in the Greater Horn of Africa." *USAID*.

Weiss, L. 1987. "Explaining the underground economy, state, and social structure." *Journal of British Sociology*, 32(2), 216–234.

Whitbeck, L. and D. Hoyt. 1999. *Nowhere to Grow*. New York: Aldine de Gruyter.

Whitbeck, L. and R. Simons. 1990. "Life on the Streets: The Victimization of Runaway and Homeless Adolescents." *Youth and Society*, 22(1), 108–215.

Whitchurch, G. and L. Constantine. 1993. "Systems Theory," in P. G. Boss, W. J. Doherty, R. LaRossa, W. R. Schumm, and S. K. Steinmetz, eds., *Sourcebook of Family Theories and Methods: A Contextual Approach*. New York: Plenum, pp. 325–352.

Williamson, J. 1989. "What Washington Means by Policy Reform," in J. Williamson, ed., *Latin American Adjustment: How Much has Happened?* Washington, DC: Institute for International Economics.

———, ed. 1989. *Latin American Adjustment: How Much has Happened?* Washington, DC: Institute for International Economics.

World Bank. 1981. *Accelerated Development in Sub-Saharan Africa.* Washington, DC: World Bank.

———. 1984. *Ghana: Policies and Program for Adjustment.* Washington, D.C.: World Bank.

———. 1989. *Sub-Saharan Africa: From Crisis to Sustainable Growth.* Washington, D.C.: World Bank.

———. 2008. *World Development Report, 2008. Agriculture for Development.* Washington D.C.: World Bank.

———. 2008. *World Bank's List of Heavily Indebted Poor Countries* (41 countries). http://go.worldbank.org/4IMVXTQ090. Accessed March 3, 2008.

World Health Organization. 2000. "Mental Health Determinants and Populations." Department of Mental Health and Substance Dependence. Geneva.

Yadava, K. 1988. *Determinants, Patterns and Consequences of Rural-Urban Migration in India.* Delhi: Independent Publishing Company.

Yeboah, I. 2000. "Structural Adjustment and Emerging Urban Form in Accra, Ghana." *Africa Today*, 47, 61–89.

Yeboah, I. and N. Waters. 1997. "Urban Economic Participation and Survival Strategies in Ghana: 1960–1984." *Tijdschrift voor Economische en Sociale Geografie*, 88, 353–368.

Yoder, K., L. Whitbeck and D. Hoyt. 2001. "Event History Analysis of Antecedents to Running Away from Home and Being on the Street." *American Behavioral Scientist*, 45(1), 51–65.

Younger, S. 1989. *Ghana: Economic Recovery Program: A Case Study of Stabilization and Structural Adjustment in Sub-Saharan Africa. Successful Development in Africa – Case Studies of Projects, Programs, and Policies.* Economic Development Institute of the World Bank analytical case study #1. Washington, DC: World Bank.

Index

Vivian Amantana

Dr. Vivian Amantana is an Associate Professor in the Department of Criminal Justice at Western Oregon University in Monmouth, Oregon. Dr. Amantana holds a Ph.D. in Family Studies and Sociology from Oregon State University in Corvallis.